EFFECTIVE
MARRIAGE
COUNSELING

Other books by Willard F. Harley, Jr.

His Needs, Her Needs
Love Busters
Five Steps to Romantic Love
Surviving an Affair
Fall in Love, Stay in Love
His Needs, Her Needs for Parents

EFFECTIVE MARRIAGE COUNSELING

The *His Needs, Her Needs* Guide
to Helping Couples

WILLARD F. HARLEY, JR.

R
Revell

a division of Baker Publishing Group
Grand Rapids, Michigan

© 2010 by Willard F. Harley, Jr.

Published by Revell
a division of Baker Publishing Group
P.O. Box 6287, Grand Rapids, MI 49516-6287
www.revellbooks.com

Printed in the United States of America

Library of Congress Cataloging-in-Publication Data
Harley, Willard F.
  Effective marriage counseling : the his needs, her needs guide to helping couples / Willard F. Harley, Jr.
      p.   cm.
  Includes bibliographical references (p.   ) and index.
  ISBN 978-0-8007-1945-6 (cloth)
  1. Marriage counseling. 2. Pastoral counseling. I. Title.
BV4012.27.H37 2010
259′.14—dc22   2009036945

10   11   12   13   14   15   16   7   6   5   4   3   2   1

Contents

Part 1 Theory: The Harley Model for Marital Satisfaction

1. A Simple and Effective Model   9
2. The Basic Assumption: The Love Bank   15
3. What Does a Good Marriage Counselor Do?   23
4. What Is Marriage Coaching?   33

Part 2 Method: Building Love Bank Balances

5. Love Bank Deposits for Men   49
6. Love Bank Deposits for Women   65
7. The Policy of Undivided Attention   79
8. Control and Abuse   89
9. Dishonesty and Annoying Behavior   101
10. Independent Behavior and the Policy of Joint Agreement   109

Part 3 Application: A Case Study

11. Intake and Assessment   121
12. Treatment   137
13. Practice and Discharge   149

Appendix A: Love Bank Inventory   167
Appendix B: Memorandum of Agreement   173
Appendix C: Telephone Counseling   179
Notes   181
Index   183

PART 1

THEORY

The Harley Model for Marital Satisfaction

1

A Simple and Effective Model

Throughout recorded history, scientists have tried to understand our universe—and everything in it—by creating models that predict future events. They assume that they understand the present correctly if they are able to accurately predict the future. Predictability is, and has always been, an essential ingredient of a good scientific model, and the model that best predicts the future is the model that's generally recognized as superior.

But there's a second rule scientists use in creating models: the simpler the better. If two models both predict the future accurately, but one requires fewer assumptions, the simpler one wins.

One of the most cited applications of this rule can be found in models of planetary motion. In the second century AD, Ptolemy created a model of planetary motion in which the Earth was the center of the solar system. Fifteen centuries later, Copernicus put forth a system where the sun was the center. Amazingly enough, both models accurately predicted planetary motion, but Ptolemy used more assumptions and much more complex mathematical formulas than those used by Copernicus.

Today we can observe the Earth rotating around the sun from satellites, but in the days of Copernicus, it was the simplicity of his model that convinced scientists that it was the best.

The Science of Marital Satisfaction

I've spent most of my adult lifetime trying to understand marital satisfaction. What must a couple do to be happily married? And what are the fewest assumptions necessary to accurately predict that outcome? In other words, what is the simplest model I could find to successfully predict marital satisfaction?

I had a special advantage over most other scientists studying the same topic. I was experiencing marital satisfaction. My wife, Joyce, and I have been happily married for more than forty-seven years. Furthermore, my parents were also happily married, as were Joyce's parents. What had all of us done to make our marriages successful? And what was the simplest way to express it?

All scientists begin with assumptions based on observation and common sense, and that's where I started as well. I began with assumptions used by my father, who was also a psychologist and marriage counselor.

My father counseled couples directly from the Bible, using various texts to encourage them to love each other sacrificially and unconditionally. He thought that his sacrificial and unconditional love for my mother is what made their marriage successful, and that assumption was one of the foundations of his counseling model.

Commitment in marriage was another basic ingredient for a successful marriage, according to my father. Once married, a couple was forever married from God's perspective. If a couple was committed to each other for life, my father believed, their marriage would be more successful.

My father's approach to marriage counseling might have helped some couples to improve their marriages in the 40s and 50s. But it was 1960 when I had my first marriage counseling experience. I was only nineteen and not yet married, but a friend in college wanted my advice. He had been married for only a few months, and it was not going well. So just as my father had done with so many couples, I stressed commitment, unconditional love, and personal sacrifice as the basic elements of a successful marriage.

By the end of the year, my friend was divorced.

Changing Times

I was about to witness a change in our culture that would threaten the nuclear family for decades to come. The value of selflessness was being replaced by selfishness. The "Me Generation" had been born.

My efforts to convince couples that they should learn selflessness and be committed to each other for life didn't work. In almost every couple I counseled, there was at least one spouse who felt that selflessness and commitment made no sense at all. That spouse wanted out. And in most cases, the other spouse wasn't in the mood to be selfless or committed after being the victim of neglect, abuse, infidelity, and other indignities. Even the pastor of my church, whose wife had an affair with the choir director, wouldn't follow my advice to "return evil with good." He heaped abuse on his wife until she finally divorced him.

But couples' lack of motivation to be selfless wasn't the only problem. In the course of my counseling, I was able to come across a few people who really did try to be selfless and committed to their marriage, and even then it didn't always work. The unconditional love of a neglected wife usually left her permanently neglected. The forgiving husband of an unfaithful wife was often the victim of yet another affair. And abused spouses experienced increased danger of abuse when they tried to respond with selfless love.

I was baffled. I couldn't motivate most couples to do the right thing, but even those I *did* motivate didn't have an improved relationship. Since I concluded I was not cut out for the job, I stopped offering marital advice for a while.

After I had earned a PhD in psychology in 1967 and become a college professor, couples kept asking me to help them with their marriages. I wanted to but I knew my skills and assumptions were inadequate. So I decided to become formally trained in the most successful method of marital therapy I could find.

The model I used was very popular at the time and still is. It was based on the assumption that marital satisfaction grew from effective conflict resolution. If a couple would learn to resolve their conflicts the right way, their marriages would be successful.

So I was trained to teach couples communication skills. They would learn to listen to each other and to respect each other's opinions. Eventually their discussions would lead to common ground and their conflicts would be resolved. This model fit the perspective of a selfish generation, because it focused attention on learning how to get what you want in marriage.

And some couples *were* helped by this technique. But even as I became increasingly successful in helping couples communicate effectively, I also witnessed incontrovertible evidence that good communication in marriage was *not* the magic bullet. Some of the couples I counseled learned to communicate better than Joyce and I ever would, but they still ended up divorced. In fact the clinic director, who created the program and taught me how to counsel this way, was divorced by his wife shortly after I completed my internship.

By this time, Joyce and I had been happily married for thirteen years. During those years I had completed a PhD program, we had two children, we had moved ten times, and Joyce's father had died unexpectedly. Yet through it all, we were still in love. What kept our marriage successful when others were failing at an unprecedented rate in 1975?

Changing the Model

There were several assumptions I could have made regarding the reasons for my marital success. We were committed to each other for life, we loved each other unconditionally, and we were willing to sacrifice our happiness for each other. We also communicated well. But my counseling experience had taught me that these conditions didn't necessarily guarantee success. So what else might it be? And how could I use this information to save marriages?

I went right to the source of the problem—couples who were in trouble—and I asked them questions. Why were they divorcing? And what would it take to turn their marriages around?

I was looking for something beyond their lack of commitment, their lack of willingness to sacrifice, and their poor communication skills. And eventually I found it. Time and time again they told me that the reason they were divorcing was they had lost their feeling of love for each other. Couple after couple said they were unwilling to remain in a loveless marriage. I would ask, "If you were in love again, would you reconsider?" Most said they might but they didn't believe anything could restore their love.

Here was a perspective I hadn't considered. I had assumed that the feeling of love that Joyce and I had for each other (which I later called "romantic love") was the *result* of our commitment and sacrificial love. Could it be the *cause*? Were we committed *because* we were in love? Were we willing to sacrifice *because* of our feelings toward each other?

There was an easy way to test this hypothesis. I could teach couples how to fall in love with each other. If romantic love was the cause of a successful marriage, when a marriage counselor taught a couple to fall in love, the marriage would become fulfilling. The couple would then report having a renewed commitment and willingness to sacrifice for each other.

A search of the current literature and consultation with many marital therapists provided no encouragement for my new model. Loss of romantic love had never been seriously considered as a cause for divorce. In fact literally every professional therapist I consulted told me that romantic love could not survive in marriage. They told me that it would last only a few months, maybe as long as three years into a marriage at best. So if a couple wanted a successful marriage, they would have to accept the loss of love as being natural and inevitable. To assume anything else was an illusion, they believed.

Well then, what was wrong with Joyce and me? We'd been married thirteen years and *we* were still in love. Had we set a world record? Not possible, since my parents were also still in love, and they'd been married more than thirty-five years. When professional therapists told me romantic love could not be sustained, I knew they were wrong.

To make a long story short, over a period of two years, I learned how to create the feeling of love in couples who had lost that feeling.

I even designed a test to measure romantic love and have been using that test ever since. My history of failure as a marriage counselor turned into a future of success.

I've written this book to explain how you can also save marriages by helping couples create and sustain their love for each other. Whether you are a student taking a course in marital therapy, a marital therapist, a clergyman who counsels troubled couples, or simply a concerned layman who knows a couple who is about to divorce, I want to show you how you can be just as successful as I've been. In the rest of this book, I'll explain the model I've developed and will describe some of the techniques that derive from this model.

My lifetime goal has been to save as many marriages as I can. For this reason I want to help you learn to use a model that's both the simplest and most effective for predicting marital satisfaction, one that's proven to be successful when it's followed, and one that will show you how to help couples fall in love and stay in love.

2

The Basic Assumption

The Love Bank

My model for marital satisfaction has only one basic assumption: almost everything a husband and wife do affects each other either positively or negatively, and that effect determines the feelings they have for each other. If they affect each other positively enough and avoid affecting each other too negatively, they will be in love with each other. This assumption is best illustrated by an analogy I created—the Love Bank.

Within each of us is a place that records the effect that others have on us. I call this place the Love Bank, and everyone we encounter has his or her own personal account in it. When we have a positive encounter with someone, love units are deposited into his or her account in our Love Bank. When we have a negative encounter, love units are withdrawn.

> **One Basic Assumption:** Almost everything a husband and wife do affects each other either positively or negatively, and that effect determines the feelings they have for each other. If they affect each other positively enough and avoid affecting each other too negatively, they will be in love with each other.

Our reactions to a person accumulate over time and create either a positive or a negative balance, depending on the total number of deposits and withdrawals the person has made. When we have more positive than negative reactions to someone, his or her balance in our Love Bank will be positive. But if we associate someone with more negative reactions, his or her balance will be negative.

Our emotions interpret the balance found in each account and produce feelings for the person who created the balance. If someone's balance is positive, we "like" the person; if it's negative, we "dislike" the person. But if the balance is particularly high (or low), exceptional feelings are triggered. A very high balance that breaches what I call the "romantic love threshold" creates the feeling of love. A very low balance that drops below the "hate threshold" triggers the feeling of hatred.

Romantic Love Threshold: A very high Love Bank balance that triggers the feeling of romantic love.

Conditioned Reflexes

The basic assumption of my model for marital satisfaction was influenced by a conditioning model of learning first explained by Ivan P. Pavlov.[1] In his famous demonstration, he was able to show that when a dog's salivation (unconditioned response) was triggered by food (unconditioned stimulus), the pairing of a bell (conditioned stimulus) with the food and salivation would eventually result in the bell alone triggering salivation (conditioned response).

Using this model as a basic reference, I predicted that when someone does something (unconditioned stimulus) that creates good feelings (unconditioned response) in another person, the person alone (conditioned stimulus) could eventually trigger the good feelings (conditioned response). If the association was strong enough, it would trigger romantic love. The association of bad feelings would have the same effect, but it would be negative.

I tested my basic assumption of the Love Bank for about ten years before I first described it in my book *His Needs, Her Needs.*[2] I found that it worked to perfection. Since then, many others have also used this assumption as the basis for their own models, and when applied correctly it has worked well for those therapists too.

There are some who borrow only part of the assumption, though, and that can get them into trouble. One common problem is to focus only on positive balances and to ignore negative balances. But we all know that withdrawals in marriage can continue to occur indefinitely, long after all deposits have been exhausted. And when that happens, not only do spouses stop loving each other but they start disliking each other. If withdrawals continue, they can come to hate each other.

That's the reason I put as much emphasis on understanding *negative* Love Bank balances as I do on understanding *positive* balances. When I first see couples for counseling, most of them are suffering from negative balances. Instead of feeling committed and willing to love unconditionally, the way spouses with high Love Bank balances feel, they are uncommitted and unwilling to do anything for each other. If a counselor does not know how to treat the state of mind that is created by negative balances, there's little chance for marital recovery.

The Practices of Unhappy Couples

My goal for every couple is to raise their Love Bank balances beyond the romantic love threshold. But negative Love Bank balances make couples very difficult to treat. Even though my program of marital recovery works when it's actually followed, couples in an unhappy marriage usually don't feel like following it. They don't feel like being nice—they feel like being mean. So instead of wanting to make each other happy, they want to make each other unhappy.

In other words, a couple in an unhappy marriage is in a negative feedback loop. The more withdrawals a couple makes to each other's Love Bank, the more they feel like making more withdrawals. This helps explain why bad marriages

Negative Feedback Loop in an Unhappy Marriage: The more withdrawals a couple makes to each other's Love Bank, the more they feel like making more withdrawals.

can get so abusive and dangerous before a divorce. Instead of trying to heal the relationship, spouses do what they can to hurt each other with greater effort and imagination.

So you will need to learn how to motivate a couple to make Love Bank deposits when they don't feel like being nice. And you'll also have to keep them from making Love Bank withdrawals when they feel like being mean.

Scientific Evidence

It's very difficult to prove that one model of marital satisfaction is superior to another. The ultimate test is to assign couples randomly to various models and to measure their marital satisfaction after the provisions of each model have been implemented.

But the training of therapists is a huge problem. How can we be sure that the therapist assigned to each model was properly trained? And there's also the problem of representation and random assignment. Does the group of volunteer couples represent the population at large? And is the assignment to treatment groups really random? Then there's the ethical problem of assigning couples to a control group where they receive no effective treatment. When they divorce, does the researcher bear any responsibility? Finally, if someone who has a stake in the outcome does the research, it usually shows that his or her approach is best. Shouldn't studies of alternative models of marital satisfaction be conducted by those neutral to the outcome?

My own personal experience led me to the model I've been using for the past thirty-five years, but that's not proof of its superiority over other models. What I need is objective studies, conducted by those who have no bias, that compare this model to others. Such studies are hard to find, even among those who have published hundreds of articles on marital therapy.

But I can direct you to three studies that support my enthusiasm. They all deal with my book *His Needs, Her Needs*, the popular application of my model, and the effect it has on couples who read it.

In a way, it's like helping someone lose weight. We all know that eating less and exercising more causes weight loss. That simple model is all you need to know. But the problem that all weight loss specialists face is that their clients don't want to eat less and they don't want to exercise more. So the challenge is to motivate people to do the right thing when they don't feel like doing it.

Measurement of Love Bank Balances

How will you know if your counseling is successful? Will a couple fall in love if they follow your plan? When they're in love, will they

---

The readers of *Marriage Partnership* magazine were asked which self-help book on marriage helped their marriages the most. In that survey *His Needs, Her Needs* came out on top. I didn't even know that the survey was being conducted, so when I called the editor after the results came in, I was curious to know more. He told me not only that it was the top choice, but it was far ahead of second place.[3]

In a national survey that I sponsored, people were asked if any self-help book on marriage solved their marital problems. Out of fifty-seven books that were read, only three were reported to have actually solved marital problems. The three were the Bible, James Dobson's *Love for a Lifetime*, and *His Needs, Her Needs*.[4]

Finally, a dissertation on the effect of self-help books on marriage supported the value of reading *His Needs, Her Needs*. Five out of six couples who read it were found to experience significant improvement in marital satisfaction.[5]

Granted, these findings are not conclusive evidence that the model I use is superior to every other model of marital satisfaction. But when you find one that works for every couple that actually follows it, you have to be impressed. And coming as I did from almost zero effectiveness to almost complete success, I can't begin to tell you how convinced I am that it's the solution to a very difficult problem we face in our society.

---

be happily married? The only way to know the answers to these questions is to have a reasonably accurate measure of romantic love.

In 1975 I asked college students to rate on a Likert scale hundreds of statements dealing with the way they felt toward someone they were dating. Then I correlated the ratings to each statement with the validity statement, "I am in love with (*the dating companion*)." The twenty items that correlated highest with that statement were used in my test. Over the years I've found this short test to be an invaluable tool in helping me evaluate my marriage counseling effectiveness. This test, the *Love Bank Inventory*, is in appendix A, and you have my permission to copy it for use in your practice.

I ask spouses to complete this test every month to help me determine their progress. If my methods are working, their scores increase each month until they're in love. If their scores don't increase, I modify the method or change my motivational approach.

There are other measures of marital satisfaction that you may have used, but I've found that most are too long to be practical. Generally spouses are unwilling to complete them often enough to measure progress. My very brief test is reasonably accurate yet can be completed quickly.

It goes without saying that you should always use some measure of progress when you are helping couples. Otherwise, you will have no way to know if the methods you are using are effective. Very well-intentioned marriage counselors spend their entire career failing to save marriages simply because they don't know that the methods they use are failing.

A simple test like the *Love Bank Inventory* will not only demonstrate your effectiveness but will also shed light on ineffective methods, helping you throw them on the scrap heap where they belong.

Effective Treatment Strategies from One Basic Assumption

The basic assumption of the Love Bank creates the therapeutic objective of romantic love between spouses. That, in turn, leads to treatment strategies that are designed to help a couple build their Love Bank accounts by creating positive associations and avoiding negative associations. Since progress can be determined by measuring changes in the emotional feelings spouses have toward each other (I normally measure those feelings once a month for spouses I counsel), a therapist can regularly evaluate the effectiveness of any treatment strategy.

By asking hundreds of spouses what it would take to make them the happiest, I discovered the best ways for couples to make Love Bank deposits. From these interviews, I found that a list of ten categories covered almost all of the responses I received. I'll describe these categories that I later called "emotional needs" in chapters 5–7. I will also briefly summarize how I usually teach couples to meet them for each other.

But as I mentioned earlier, I give equal attention to helping couples avoid making Love Bank withdrawals. In those same interviews with couples, I also discovered six ways that spouses make each other miserable. I called those categories Love Busters. I'll describe them to you and show you how to teach couples to avoid them in chapters 8–10. With these tools you can go to work helping couples restore their love for each other.

In chapters 11–13 I'll describe a case study that puts theory and method into practice. It will take you all the way from intake to discharge with a detailed accounting of how I apply my model of marital satisfaction to a couple.

Before I explain the methods I use to help couples build Love Bank accounts and how I apply them in practice, I'll describe in the next chapter some generally accepted characteristics of a good marriage counselor. Then in chapter 4, I'll focus attention on one of those characteristics that is particularly important—the ability to motivate.

3

What Does a Good Marriage Counselor Do?

For fifteen years, as director of a large network of mental health clinics, one of my primary responsibilities was to train and evaluate mental health therapists. In this chapter I'll describe my training goals for marriage counselors. They have to do with three categories that I call *emotional minefields, uncreative wilderness,* and *apathetic swamps.* Good marriage counselors know how to guide couples through these obstacles.

Obstacles to a Good Marriage

Emotional minefields represent the predictable yet overwhelmingly painful experiences that many couples go through as they try to adjust to each other. Hurt feelings are the most common result, but depression, anger, panic, paranoia, and many other emotions seem to pop up without

> **Emotional Minefields:** The predictable yet overwhelmingly painful experiences that many couples go through as they try to adjust to each other.

warning. These emotions distract couples from their goal of creating a successful marriage and often sabotage the entire effort.

Good marriage counselors help couples avoid many of these emotional land mines and are there for damage control when they're triggered. They understand the enormous stress couples are under as they are facing one of their greatest crises. When one or both spouses become emotionally upset, good marriage counselors have the skill to calm them down and assure them that their emotional reactions are not a sign of hopeless incompatibility.

The *creative wilderness* represents the typical inability of couples in marital crisis to create effective solutions to their problems. Their state of mind encourages them to do the opposite of what would work. Instead of a desire to care for each other, they are often hostile. When asked, "What would make you happy?" they respond with wanting to see less of each other. They are often unwilling to meet each other's important emotional needs, especially intimate needs.

> *Creative Wilderness:* The typical inability of couples in marital crisis to create effective solutions to their problems.

Good marriage counselors are a valuable resource for effective strategies and they know how to apply them. They offer advice that is often contrary to what a couple really wants to do because they know it works. In the chapters on method, I'll tell you about some of my most successful plans for marital recovery.

By taking advantage of special training programs that address common marital problems, good marriage counselors continue to build their inventory of effective strategies throughout their lives. If you learn how and when to use this training, you'll provide the expertise and experience couples should expect in a good marriage counselor.

Apathetic swamps represent the feeling of discouragement that most couples experience. They may feel that any effort to improve their marriage is a waste of time. And discouragement is contagious. When one spouse is discouraged, the other quickly follows. Encouragement, on the other hand, may be met with skepticism by the other spouse. So it's easy for a couple to be discouraged, and difficult to be encouraged, while trying to solve their marital problems.

Good marriage counselors know how to provide needed encouragement, and their clients know that at least their counselor believes that their effort will be successful. Eventually each spouse comes to believe it too.

> *Apathetic Swamps:* The feeling of discouragement that most couples experience.

But good marriage counselors do more than just encourage their clients—they also motivate them to follow the plan that leads to their recovery. In the next chapter I'll focus special attention on how you can motivate couples to restore their love for each other when they come to you feeling apathetic. I call it *coaching* rather than *counseling*, because all too often counseling has been associated with a passive, nondirective approach to problem solving. Coaching, on the other hand, is assertive and directive. A coach helps clients set goals and sees to it that they are achieved.

A Good Marriage Counselor's Sequence of Therapy

The three characteristics of a good marriage counselor that I've just described can be realized only in the context of a logical therapeutic sequence. The sequence that I highly recommend to you is intake, assessment, treatment, practice, and discharge.

> *Coaching:* Being assertive and directive, a coach helps clients set goals and sees to it that they are achieved.

The First Session—Intake

Making the first appointment with a marriage counselor is a huge hurdle for most couples. At least one spouse may be reluctant, and often they have heard horror stories from those who found that marriage counselors did more harm than good. A 1995 *Consumer Reports* study rated marriage counseling dead last in effectiveness when comparing various types of psychotherapy.[6] So a couple's hesitant effort to get the help they need should be met with encouragement, and that encouragement should begin at the moment of their inquiry.

When a couple calls for their first appointment, they typically have questions that should be answered. I have encouraged every counselor who worked under my supervision to be willing to talk directly by telephone to a prospective couple (without charge) to answer questions such as:

How many years have you been a counselor?

What are your credentials (for example, academic degree)?

What is the cost?

How many sessions will be needed?

How often will we be seen?

Do you help your clients avoid some of the emotional hazards of marital adjustment?

Do you suggest strategies to solve your clients' marital problems?

Do you help motivate your clients to complete the program successfully?

During this precounseling inquiry, you should communicate compassion for the couple and confidence that a solution will be found. A couple should be able to briefly explain to you what type of marital problem they face and they should learn about special training or experience you've had in solving that problem. If you are unable to speak directly with couples for some reason, someone in your office should be able to give couples the information they need to make a good decision.

If a couple sees you in a clinic or church, a receptionist should be present and the waiting room should be pleasant and relaxing. The couple should register at the desk when they arrive and be asked to complete registration forms, insurance forms (if you qualify for third-party payments), and contracts. They should be encouraged to read these forms carefully before signing them. The receptionist should also carefully explain confidentiality policies.

Most "hour" sessions are actually forty-five minutes long. Counselors need fifteen minutes to complete notes and prepare for the next session. While I've tried to time my sessions carefully, I am flexible and considerate at the end of each hour. Sometimes I find myself giving a couple extra time to pull themselves together before they leave.

Punctuality is very important. When a counselor always runs late, it's a very disrespectful way to treat a couple. Their time is important, and they shouldn't be expected to waste it waiting for you. With the extra fifteen minutes between sessions, each couple can be seen on time.

Most marriage counselors see spouses together for the entire first session, but I am extremely opposed to that policy. Instead, I see each person separately for fifteen minutes so that I can gain their individual perspectives. During that time they have the opportunity to complain about each other without making matters worse. Then I see them together for the remainder of the session where I explain the next step, which is the assessment.

Don't ever give spouses an opportunity to argue with each other while they are in your presence. Remember, you want to teach them how to make Love Bank deposits and avoid withdrawals. For their comfort and security, let them know that when they are together in your office, they are to avoid saying anything that could be interpreted as being disrespectful or argumentative.

The purpose of the first session is for you to meet the couple and for them to become familiar with you. There should be absolutely no suggestion from you as to how you plan to solve their problem—only that you will lay out a plan for them after they've completed the assessment. During the first session, you are there to encourage them.

There are six assessment forms that I send home with the couple. Each spouse is to complete each form. These forms are:

1. *Emotional Needs Questionnaire* (ENQ)
2. *Love Busters Questionnaire* (LBQ)
3. *Marital Problems Analysis* (MPA)
4. *Personal History Questionnaire* (PHQ)
5. *Marital Counseling History Questionnaire* (MCHQ)
6. *Love Bank Inventory* (LBI)

You have my permission to use all of these forms at no charge. You may download the first five from the Marriage Builders website (marriagebuilders.com) in the "Questionnaires" section. The sixth, *Love Bank Inventory*, is in this book in appendix A.

In the chapters that follow, I'll refer to a number of other forms that I use in my counseling practice to help couples create and implement a plan for recovery. It wasn't possible to include all of them in this book. Many of them can be downloaded free of charge from the questionnaires section of my website. All are available in *Five Steps to Romantic Love: A Workbook for Readers of* Love Busters *and* His Needs, Her Needs. Other resources that will be of particular value to you are my books *His Needs, Her Needs: Building an Affair-Proof Marriage* and *Love Busters: Protecting Your Marriage from Habits That Destroy Romantic Love.*[7]

I encourage both spouses to set aside five hours to complete these forms. In some cases they schedule the time while still in my office. I instruct them to complete them separately and to avoid looking at each other's answers. They'll have an opportunity to see most of their spouse's answers at their assessment during the second session.

The program of recovery that I use requires fifteen hours of a couple's time each week. I warn them that after the assessment, if they do not schedule that amount of time to complete the assignments, I will not be able to help them.

For the most part, advice should be avoided during the intake session, because at this point goals and a treatment plan are not yet determined. But I do suggest advising the couple to avoid arguing about anything while they are at home together during the next week.

The second appointment should be scheduled for no more than a week later. If possible, the couple should be assessed within a few days. This is because they are usually suffering from their problems and would like relief as soon as possible. If your schedule is too full to allow a quick assessment, you should refer the couple to a qualified counselor who can accommodate them.

The Second Session—Assessment

The purpose of the second session is to review the forms the couple completed and to create treatment goals. As a rule, it takes me three hours to complete this session—one hour individually with each spouse and one hour together to formally agree to goals, which are carefully described in writing.

The results of every form, except the *Love Bank Inventory*, should be revealed to both spouses. This will help them come to an informed decision regarding their goals. Explain to both spouses that the *Love Bank Inventory* is for your eyes only so that you can evaluate the effectiveness of the treatment plan you will use to achieve these goals. I've found that these scores are too sensitive to reveal to a couple, especially when the responses are negative.

There's no point to treatment until goals are set, but poorly organized counselors will often see clients for weeks before they get down to deciding what they hope to accomplish. During this time, the crisis that prompted a couple to seek counseling may pass and a couple's motivation to solve the underlying problem may wane until the next crisis. As a result, the couple drops out of therapy, no wiser or better off than when they came. To avoid this tragic end, you should focus on goals immediately, while the couple is still motivated to do something about their problem.

The form I use to describe therapeutic goals is the *Memorandum of Agreement* (MOA), which is provided for your use in appendix B. It is a general statement of long-term objectives that flow from the assessment.

The MOA spells out clearly the most urgent goals that are to be achieved, in most cases, within the next eight sessions. The ENQ, the LBQ, and the MPA are my primary sources for these goals, because they identify the most urgent problems. In the MPA, a rating of 1 is assigned to issues that threaten the marriage unless resolved. After the eight sessions when those urgent goals are achieved, the couple can then decide if they need my help to achieve other goals. In many cases, the couple can take it from there without my assistance.

Part III C of the *Memorandum of Agreement* requires couples to give each other undivided attention for a minimum of fifteen hours a week. The time a couple spends together is like a blank canvas. What they do together is the painting. Without the canvas, there's no place to paint. To help a couple learn to schedule this time together, they use a form I provide, the *Time for Undivided Attention Worksheet*. I ask them to schedule the time together in advance and then document how they use the time on the worksheet. While they are in counseling, most of these fifteen hours are to be spent completing the lesson assignments I give them.

At the end of the second session, the couple should be given a lesson assignment designed to treat the most important problem they face. It should be made clear to the couple that you expect compliance and that if they don't complete the assignment, they are wasting their time and money. The value of marriage counseling is in what is achieved between sessions, not necessarily what is achieved during the session. They are to be reminded of their next appointment one or two days before its scheduled time and asked if their assignment has been completed. If it is not completed, the appointment should be postponed. Couples who come to your office having failed to complete their assignments must be treated with respect but also with firmness. If you have a treatment plan that always works when followed (like the one I'll be describing in the following chapters), lack of motivation will be your greatest barrier to success.

In chapter 11, Intake and Assessment, I describe in detail how I take a couple through this phase of the counseling process. It will give you a much clearer vision of how my assessment forms and procedures are used in practice.

Treatment and Practice

Beginning with the third session, treatment plans that help couples achieve goals they set should be implemented and evaluated. Assignments should be given at each session and the couple's success or failure in following the assignments reported at the next session. Your notes should reflect this dynamic. If your plan is effective, and you are able to guide the couple through the emotional minefields, uncreative wilderness, and apathetic swamps, you will see improvement almost immediately. This improvement will be reflected in the results of the *Love Bank Inventory* that each spouse should complete every month.

After a treatment plan has been introduced, practice is required to turn the new behaviors into established habits. Generally I recommend that a new treatment plan for one of the goals be introduced each session, while the couple continues to practice behavior that achieves other goals introduced in earlier sessions. As a rule, I do not try to tackle more than three goals at a time. A description of how this actually works is found in chapter 12.

Expect progress to occur in fits and starts. Some weeks will be blissful while others can be unbearable for the couple. If the *Love Bank Inventory* is completed after a particularly bad week, it may seem that the overall plan is not working. Using this instrument along with knowledge of the situation will help you differentiate between a temporary setback and a failing treatment plan.

It's common for couples to experience a crisis between appointments that requires a counselor's timely mediation. In most cases I've been willing to let couples call me at the office or at home for emergencies because I realize that I'm working with people in crisis. And this privilege has rarely been abused. Even with hundreds of current clients at a time, I've always found that they have been very respectful of my privacy. Sometimes a call is simply for clarification of an assignment. But there have also been threats of suicide, violent arguments, and irresponsible behavior that need to be dealt with at the time they occur. If I get a call from a couple, I usually schedule their appointments closer together.

When Should a Couple Be Discharged?

As marital problems are solved, couples should be seen less often. I use no hard-and-fast rule for scheduling, but normally I begin with a session each week, and end with the sessions being six months apart, just to check on a couple's status. Ordinarily there are eight treatment sessions that span about two years.

A counselor I was supervising recently told me about a breakthrough with a couple he was seeing. They had come to him with the husband's complaint that his wife was not making love to him often enough. After a few weeks of counseling, she made love to her husband so many times during a weekend that the husband finally cried "uncle." The counselor was ready to discharge them, but my advice was to continue counseling them on a less frequent basis. One passionate weekend did not necessarily mean that their problem was solved.

Generally men want to get out of therapy as soon as possible, even when they were the one who wanted it the most in the beginning.

They don't like the idea of reporting to someone regarding their behavior, and my role as a counselor is to see to it that they follow through on what they promised. After agreeing to anything to get their wives to meet their needs or return home, once she's complied, they often go back to their old habits.

With this type of problem in mind, encourage couples to continue therapy until they both enthusiastically agree to end it. If one of them, frequently the wife, wants to keep the door open, they can be scheduled once every six months just in case the old problems resurface.

In the end, the results of the *Love Bank Inventories* and the couple's corroborating admission will determine if they are in love with each other, which is the ultimate test of your success. When test results are consistently above a score of 1.8 (what I consider to be the romantic love threshold), and the behavior of the couple reinforces the score, I discharge a couple.

But in some cases, even though I no longer counsel a couple, I encourage them to send me *Love Bank Inventories* once or twice a year. It's a good way to stop Love Bank balances from eroding too far before a correction is made. Remember what I said about positive versus negative balances. It's easy for couples to make Love Bank deposits when balances are positive, but very difficult to make them when the balances are negative.

My experience with thousands of couples I have counseled personally, and tens of thousands more I have known through supervision, has led me to the conclusion that most marriage counseling can be successful in about ten sessions, over a period of about two years, when couples have followed the treatment plan I've recommended. But not all couples follow the treatment plan on a regular basis, and this can lead to a lengthening of the time for their recovery.

As I mentioned earlier, if you have a treatment plan that works when followed, your greatest barrier to success is lack of motivation. So in the next chapter I'll describe some of the motivational tools I've used to coach couples to follow treatment plans that work.

4

What Is Marriage Coaching?

I was raised in a Germanic tradition of "no pain, no gain." Many, if not most, of my childhood achievements were accomplished through personal sacrifice and hard work. During my adolescence and then later as an adult, I applied the rule of personal sacrifice to almost every goal I had. Without a doubt, if I had not forced myself to work long and hard, I would not have amounted to much. And that's the story of most people who have achieved their personal objectives—they must work for them.

My approach to achievement made me a natural coach. From my high school days right up to the present, I have been coaching people to do whatever it takes to be successful. Whether the goal is mastery of academic subjects, physical conditioning, career development, or . . . marriage, I have tried to help people understand that they can have what they want if they are willing to work for it.

In my ten years of teaching psychology and statistics (1967–1977), I didn't grade on the curve. Instead, I gave every student a chance to earn an A, but they had to earn it. Tests were given for every lecture and reading assignment, and students could retake them until they had a perfect score (a different test was given for each retake). Free tutoring was available to students who were having trouble learning the material. My goal was for each student to learn all of the material I presented. I did not want students to be satisfied with a *B* grade, because it would have meant that they had missed something I felt was important.

It was not unusual for students to report that they spent more time studying for my classes than for all their other classes combined. For many of them, the *A* grade they earned from me was the only one they had received in college up to that point. But after learning how to study for an *A*, from then on, they earned *A*s in many other classes. They discovered that the time and effort they spent studying was proportional to the grades they received, and so their grades improved as their overall commitment to study improved.

The approach I used to help students succeed in my psychology courses proved successful in achieving other personal objectives as well. As a clinical psychologist, I helped many overweight people lose weight and keep it off. I helped hundreds of alcoholics stop drinking and smokers stop smoking. I did it all with plans that were proven to be successful if people were willing to follow them. My job, as their coach, was to provide the plan and then motivate them to follow it. And in most cases I was motivating people to follow a plan they really didn't want to follow.

The Importance of a Coach

Whether it's getting an *A* in a psychology course, losing weight, giving up smoking, or having a great marriage, the plan that achieves personal objectives is usually something that people would rather not do, and that's the reason a coach can be so important. To quote Tom Landry, former coach of the Dallas Cowboys, the coach's job is "getting players to do what they don't want to do so they can be the kind of players they always wanted to be."

But for many people these days, marriage counseling is often more about helping couples make the most of their upcoming and inevitable divorce. Instead of trying to motivate a couple to learn how to fall in love, there's almost a deliberate effort to demonstrate that the couple should never have married in the first place and divorce is their best choice for future happiness and fulfillment.

In fact teaching the couple anything is often frowned upon. Trying to motivate them to do something they don't want to do is viewed by many as shocking—downright unethical. They feel that the role of a counselor is to help couples gain insight, create their own plan, and take responsibility for it. When this approach fails to help a couple solve their problems and save their marriage, the counselor is off the hook. They don't acknowledge that the uncreative wilderness a failing marriage imposes on a couple makes them incapable of solving their problems.

Since most counselors these days really don't have an effective plan to save a marriage, their fallback position—having couples do their own planning—makes sense. To justify their fee, they rest on the belief that a counselor is wrong to suggest a plan to a couple and then coach the couple through that plan. They deceive themselves into believing that the ethical way to counsel is to let the inner wisdom of the couple come to the rescue. When that happens, no one is actually rescued, but at least the counselor feels morally justified.

The Task of a Marriage Coach

When a couple first comes to me for counseling, one of my goals is to help them identify and meet each other's most important emotional needs so they can deposit enough love units to fall in love with each other. And I help them identify and avoid Love Busters so they stop draining each other's Love Bank accounts.

But these goals are not easy to achieve. At least one spouse usually doesn't want his or her emotional needs met and he or she doesn't want to meet the spouse's emotional needs. Instead, this person wants to hurt the spouse in the ways the spouse has hurt him or her. With almost all couples I counsel, at least one spouse is not willing to follow my plan—at first.

That's where my job as a marriage coach begins—motivating couples to do what they don't want to do so they can have the kind of marriage they want to have. I coach them in meeting each other's emotional needs and avoiding hurting each other at a time when they don't feel like doing either.

As I've already noted, most marriage counseling doesn't begin with a plan, nor does it try to motivate couples to do what they don't want to do. But marriage coaching does both. That's the reason it succeeds where most marriage counseling fails.

> **Marriage Coaching:** Motivating couples to do what they don't want to do so they can have the kind of marriage they want to have.

Are you a marriage coach? If so, you use a plan that works when it's followed and you know how to motivate couples to follow it. If this is true, you're a successful therapist and have absolutely no trouble filling your schedule with couples who need your help to save their marriages.

If you're not a marriage coach, you can be. In this book I explain the plan that always works when followed. So becoming a successful coach is a matter of learning how to motivate couples to follow the plan.

How to Motivate Couples to Do What They Don't Want to Do

For years I've taught marriage counselors how to become effective marriage coaches, and my years of experience have taught me that it's often easier to teach someone a plan that works when it's followed than it is to teach that person how to motivate spouses to follow the plan.

Sometimes I've even felt that I'd rather work with successful used car salesmen than certified marriage counselors. The salesmen already know how to motivate people—all I would need to do is teach them the program. Certified marriage counselors, on the other hand, rarely know how to motivate people. It's not included in their training. But it is possible for anyone to learn how to motivate others, and it should be a basic training requirement for all marriage counselors, because motivation is the key to success in marital therapy. It's a skill that's difficult to learn but it's absolutely necessary.

> **Motivation:** The key to success in marital therapy.

What does it take to motivate people? I will describe some of the most important characteristics of motivation. These are not inborn personality traits; they're skills that can be learned. You can become a marriage coach if you develop these skills.

Trust

The person you wish to motivate should trust you to be his or her advocate. The person must know you're on his or her side.

Trust is easiest to achieve by coaching spouses individually; so at first, I rarely coach a couple together. They come together for the session, but I talk to them separately. In a one-on-one session, I tell each spouse that I want him or her to have everything needed, and that I'll try to help the person get it. I mean every word of it. I want both spouses to be happy. As their personal advocate, I try to convince each of them to meet the other person's emotional needs and to avoid hurting each other.

Granted, one spouse is typically more at fault for the marital failure than the other spouse. But if both spouses trust me, I can expect more change from one spouse than the other. Regardless of how one-sided my recommendations may be, I can still be trusted. I'm their advocate, and they can be confident that the changes they make will ultimately be in both of their best interests.

Some counselors feel they should remain neutral to avoid the appearance of taking sides, but neutrality can convince spouses that you are not an advocate for either of them. So I do the opposite. I am passionately committed to seeing to it that both spouses have their needs met and are protected from each other's harmful behavior. I reprimand spouses who fail to achieve these objectives. Results speak for themselves, and both spouses know that they're personally benefiting from my coaching.

If you want to evaluate your coaching technique to determine if you are gaining or losing a couple's trust, I suggest you have them complete a brief feedback form that asks for that information. It should be completed after the second session (assessment) and again after every three months of counseling. In a training program, the feedback would go to your supervisor. But even if you don't have a supervisor, it can still be a valuable tool for your own personal development.

Questions you might ask are: Do you feel that I am trying to make your life better? Am I treating you fairly? What have I done to gain your trust? Have I done anything to lose your trust? When these simple questions are answered periodically, you will know how to improve your coaching methods.

Honesty

Trust and honesty have much in common. They both give the person you're trying to motivate an assurance that you have high moral standards and that your heart is in the right place. Honesty begins with the claims you make regarding your ability to help solve a couple's problems. Never exaggerate claims of your success or use illustrations that aren't real.

In the beginning of my counseling career, I was not successful in saving marriages and I told couples about my past failures before I counseled them. I didn't charge for my services either. Later, after almost all of my cases turned into great marriages, I told couples with confidence that I could save their marriage. And that's also when I started charging a fee.

Be honest with couples about your skills and the type of problems you've been particularly successful in solving. If a couple comes to you suffering from marital problems and chemical dependency, and you've had no training or success helping people overcome drug or alcohol addiction, team your case with a professional chemical dependency counselor, or refer it to someone with both marital and chemical dependency training and a history of success treating these dual problems.

Angry outbursts are another type of marital problem that require special training to treat effectively. If a couple you counsel reports a history of physical abuse, don't take the case unless you have had training and successful experience in anger management. Without training, you put an abused spouse at risk of permanent injury or even death.

Be honest in the way you coach. Don't tell spouses what they want to hear just to gain their approval. Assume that every conversation you have with each spouse will be recorded and played back to the other spouse. That way, spouses won't be able to tell each other something you've said to one that is contradicted by what you've said to the other.

The program I offer couples emphasizes radical honesty, and if I were to be the least bit dishonest, it would destroy my credibility and my ability to motivate them to follow the program.

As with trust, you can evaluate honesty with a feedback form that includes a few questions to determine if the couples you are coaching feel that you are being honest with them. Questions you might ask are: Do you feel that I am being honest with you? If so, what have I done to convince you that I'm being honest? If not, what have I done that causes you to feel I'm not being honest?

Knowledge of the Subject

A couple is more motivated to follow your advice if you have a comprehensive knowledge of marital therapy in general and knowledge of the method you use in particular. During the marital assessment, I ask couples to complete my *Marital Counseling History Questionnaire*, which also tells me the books on marriage they've read and the marriage seminars they've attended to determine what they've already experienced. Unless I know what other models of marital satisfaction they've been exposed to, I'm in no position to persuade the couple that, while they've been unsuccessful in the past, this time counseling will work.

I strongly recommend that you have a broad background in alternative approaches to marital therapy. But you should evaluate each approach critically. If saving marriages is the goal, which ones get the job done? As I stated in the first chapter, there are very few that actually save most marriages when followed. Couples who have tried and failed while using these other models should be encouraged to know that the model described in this book works when others usually fail. If you know the alternatives and why they fail, you will have an easier time convincing a couple to give their marriage one more effort.

But you'll find that alternative models of marital satisfaction are moving targets. As weaknesses are discovered, the models change, as they should. So as you try to evaluate a model this year, you may find that it's defined differently next year.

When I recently reported studies that showed one popular model actually causing a decrease in marital satisfaction after five years, compared to a no-treatment control group, I was told that recent changes addressed the problem. Today the methods used are different from those used five years earlier. For that model, continuing changes make it impossible to evaluate long-term effects.

The approach I take to saving marriages has been consistent over the past thirty-five years. That makes it easier to evaluate the long-term effect of my model and easier to address challenges that are made by others who use my quotes from the past. My ability to explain their misunderstanding in a convincing way helps give couples confidence that my program is internally consistent—that I'm not just making things up as I go along.

Some coaches who use my material are embarrassed to discover that their clients know more about it than they do. The reason the couple needs help is that they could not motivate themselves to follow a program they knew would help them. They've read a book I've written but they just can't apply what they've learned. The coach must know the program better than his or her clients, or the coach will lose a very important motivational edge.

You may add "knowledge of the subject" to your feedback form by asking the following questions: Do you feel that I have an understanding of alternative approaches to marital therapy and have chosen the method that will help you the most? If so, what have I done to convince you that it's the best approach and that I understand how it's to be applied? If you're not convinced, what have I done that causes you to doubt my knowledge of the subject?

Confidence versus Arrogance

Couples can detect the difference between confidence and arrogance after one or two sessions. Confidence motivates a couple to follow a coach's plan, but arrogance leaves them feeling they've got a fool for a coach.

There is a behavioral difference between these two that bears mentioning. A confident person doesn't appear to be bragging. He doesn't talk about himself but rather about the method he's using. An arrogant coach, however, can appear to be almost narcissistic. He or she makes it seem as if a couple is privileged to be in the presence of such a hero—more focused on his or her own reputation than on the welfare of the couple.

Another way to provide supporting evidence of your competence without appearing arrogant is to display certificates of training in clear view of couples. Documentation of your skills should be presented when a client makes a first appointment. The number of years of experience in marriage counseling should also be mentioned.

Referrals by former clients and other counselors are usually accompanied by a testimonial regarding the counselor's skill and experience. Couples who are referred come with an understanding that the counselor is especially suited to help them solve their problems. The more others say about your achievements, the more confident and less arrogant you will appear to be.

Your feedback form to determine how couples interpret your attitude can include the following questions: Do I appear to be confident in my ability? If so, what have I done to convince you that I am confident? If not, what makes you think I'm not confident? Do I appear to be arrogant to you? If so, what have I done to convince you that I am arrogant? If not, what makes you think I'm not arrogant?

Organized and Professional

I once conducted a study that investigated the effect of counseling style on clients' trust. The hypothesis I was testing predicted that warm and empathetic counselors would gain more trust than cold and distant counselors. In general, the evidence supported my hypothesis. But there was one cold and distant counselor who scored a higher level of trust than any who were warm and empathetic. His high score almost masked the truth that warmth and empathy help build trust.

Eventually, I discovered what he did that almost ruined my study—he was organized and appeared to be very professional. This counselor demonstrated that organization can trump warmth when it comes to a couple's trust. Granted, you should have both warmth and organization to ensure trust. But of the two, organization appeared to be more important in this study.

41

Be on time when you begin your session. End your session on time. Don't make couples wait for you to end a previous session. Dress for the occasion (your clothes should reflect your respect for the couple). Have an agenda for every session that is strictly followed (don't wander off on rabbit trails regarding topics you cover).

You can assess a couple's attitude about your professionalism by adding these questions to your feedback form: Do I appear to be organized and professional? If so, what have I done to convince you that I am organized and professional? If not, what makes you think I'm not organized and professional?

Accountability

Accountability is a crucial factor in marital coaching because it helps provide an ongoing measure of the success or failure of your plan. And it also motivates couples. If you don't expect a couple to follow the assignment and don't follow through to make sure they do, they generally won't.

Keep notes regarding assignments and review them in every session. Your notes should begin with the outcome of the past assignment, and should end with the new assignment. If assignments are not followed or are only partially followed, the session should be spent discussing what went wrong and how it will not happen twice.

One of the reasons that I know what works and what doesn't work in marital therapy is that I normally follow couples long after their therapy has technically ended. I continue to check in with them to be sure they are not falling back into bad habits and the plan we followed is continuing to produce positive results. By my simply observing a couple's status, they are motivated to remain faithful to the program. I've found that most of the couples I've coached find my continuing interest in them to be inspiring.

Your couples' opinion about how you've held them accountable can be investigated by asking these questions on your feedback form: Do you feel that I've held you accountable to follow the assignments I've given you? If so, what have I done to convince you that I have held you accountable? If not, what makes you think I have not held you accountable?

What Your Feedback Form Tells You

If you're a good coach who motivates your clients to follow your plan, the information on your feedback form should confirm it. Spouses should be able to tell you that they trust you, you're being honest with them, you know your subject, you're confident not arrogant, you're organized and professional, and that you're holding them accountable.

If couples tend to rate you poorly in any of these important traits, it's likely you are having difficulty motivating them. But that can change if you upgrade your ability in areas they've identified as being weak.

The ultimate measure in judging your performance is the feedback you will receive on the *Love Bank Inventory*, which measures the romantic love the spouses you coach have for each other. This is the reason measuring Love Bank accounts on a regular basis using the LBI should be part of your therapeutic plan. If this measure shows constant improvement, you're doing what you've been asked to do. But if the Love Bank quotient doesn't improve for both spouses, you're not motivating them enough. Feedback regarding each of the coaching skills I've mentioned may be in order.

Why Isn't Therapeutic Control Abusive?

A marriage coach has therapeutic control—telling spouses what to do and motivating them to do it. In marriage I view control as a form of abuse. Neither spouse should try to dominate the other because invariably it leads to massive Love Bank withdrawals. So why isn't the control I achieve as a therapist also a form of abuse?

There are many situations in life where control is warranted because romantic love is not the goal. Take the armed services, for example. Sergeants have the right to tell privates what to do. Sergeants do not need to be loved—they need privates to follow orders. Education is another example. Teachers should be able to require students to complete assignments. And counseling for everything from mental disorders to vocational planning should give experts the opportunity to guide clients to recovery—by controlling the therapeutic process.

Control is very motivating when done the right way, and the right way is to make the control voluntary. When a couple gives a coach the right to direct them toward recovery, and are willing to follow the coach's orders, the couple will see rapid improvement—if the coach's plan actually works.

When I coach a couple, I let them know from the beginning that I expect them to follow my assignments. If they fail to follow them, I focus on their failure rather than on the marital problems themselves, until they comply.

There are many schools of thought in marital therapy that judge my approach to be terribly unethical and very dangerous. But I challenge anyone to find a single example of damage to a couple that my thirty-five years of counseling has produced. Out of the thousands of couples I've treated, not a single couple has ever filed a lawsuit against me for unethical practices or has even complained that I was too controlling. Instead, I receive countless letters of appreciation for the way I have guided couples by making them do what they don't want to do so they can have the marriage they've always wanted.

Your coaching session doesn't save a marriage. It's the care that a couple learns to give each other after the session is over that does the job. Your assignment is for a couple to meet each other's emotional needs and avoid doing anything to hurt each other. Requiring a couple to follow the plan is not only ethical, it's far safer than leaving a couple to their instincts when they hate each other.

Keep Focused on the Ball

I began this book by introducing the one basic assumption that I use in therapy: if a couple makes enough deposits into and few withdrawals from each other's Love Bank account, they will be in love with each other. And once they're both in love, the risk of divorce is ended.

The Basic Assumption I Use in Therapy: If a couple makes enough deposits into and few withdrawals from each other's Love Bank account, they will be in love with each other.

When spouses have learned to make Love Bank deposits, and avoid making withdrawals, their marriages flourish. It sounds too simple to be true, but my experience has supported this conclusion tens of thousands of time. There's no need to make marriage coaching any more complicated.

There are two ingredients for successful marital therapy—a plan that works and the ability to motivate couples to follow the plan. In the next six chapters, I'll describe a plan you can use that will help couples make the largest Love Bank deposits and the fewest withdrawals. That plan, when followed, works.

PART 2

METHOD

Building Love Bank Balances

5

Love Bank Deposits for Men

How does a man fall in love with a woman? What triggers his feeling of romantic love? The Love Bank assumption points us to a general answer—enough love units to breach his romantic love threshold. But it doesn't give us any specific answer to the question, what is the fastest and easiest way to win a man's heart?

As I mentioned in chapter 2, I discovered the best ways to make Love Bank deposits by asking hundreds of married men and women to tell me what their spouse could do to make them the happiest. What made them feel very good when their spouse did it and feel very frustrated when he or she didn't? I didn't provide a list of possible answers from which they were to choose. Instead, I wanted their answers to be given without any prompts.

Almost all of the responses I recorded fell into ten categories: admiration, affection, conversation, domestic support, family commitment, financial support, honesty and openness, physical attractiveness, recreational companionship, and sexual fulfillment. I called these categories *important emotional needs* and defined an emotional need as a

> *An Emotional Need:* a craving for something that makes a person feel good when he or she has it and feel frustrated when he or she doesn't have it.

49

craving for something that makes a person feel good when he or she has it and feel frustrated when he or she doesn't have it.

After I had identified these ten needs, I asked another group of spouses to rank the needs according to how good they feel when met and how frustrated they feel when not met. I discovered that, on average, the emotional needs that were ranked in the top five by men tended to be ranked in the lowest five by women, and vice versa. I continue to collect rankings of these needs right up to this very day. And today, more than thirty-five years later, the results are the same.

Granted, there are many men and women who do not fit the average for their group. Often husbands will select one or more of their needs from the list usually associated with women. And women frequently cross over as well. Because of this, whenever I counsel a couple, I always have them complete their own ranking of needs; then I am certain I know the needs that are the most important to them.

So during the marital assessment—the second session, described in chapter 3—one of the forms I ask couples to complete is the *Emotional Needs Questionnaire*. It lists the ten important emotional needs and asks spouses to rank them. It helps them identify the ways they can make the largest deposits in each other's Love Bank.

But this initial discovery that, in general, men and women do not react the same way when a particular emotional need is met, helped me understand how difficult it would be to teach spouses to fall in love and stay in love with each other. For example, I realized that an act of affection could make a wife feel terrific, but the same act might leave the husband feeling so-so. Sex would cause massive Love Bank deposits for a husband while perhaps having little positive effect on a wife. Therefore I was faced with the daunting task of motivating spouses to do for each other something they didn't always appreciate when it was done for them.

The biblical command to "do to others as you would have them do to you" (Luke 6:31) doesn't apply when you don't want the same things. But this command can be changed without loss of meaning when it comes to marriage. Since men and women need different things from each other, we can interpret the command to read: *meet your spouse's most important emotional needs because you would want your spouse to meet yours.*

People can be motivated to follow this revised command with the guarantee that they'll get something they want for their effort. I found that one of the best ways to achieve this objective was for couples to meet each other's needs *simultaneously*. So after a couple completed the *Emotional Needs Questionnaire*, I would encourage them to make an even trade. He was to meet her two most important emotional needs and she was to meet his top two needs. When these needs were met at the same time, it encouraged them both to continue meeting these needs.

Just by meeting each other's top two emotional needs, spouses make massive Love Bank deposits and are likely to fall in love with each other. But for insurance, I encourage them to eventually get into the habit of meeting each other's top five emotional needs. This takes them so far above the romantic love threshold that the risk of losing their love for each other is negligible.

In this chapter I'll describe the five emotional needs that most men rank highest. When a woman meets these five needs, she becomes irresistible to him. I will also give you a brief summary of the training methods I use to teach wives to meet these needs. All of the forms I mention in this chapter are found in the workbook *Five Steps to Romantic Love*.

Sexual Fulfillment

The emotional need for sexual fulfillment is a craving for sexual experiences. When these experiences are provided often enough, a person with this need feels intense pleasure, and when they're not provided, he feels intense frustration. The need is caused almost entirely by the hormone testosterone, which is secreted in abundance in most men. In most cases, the more testosterone in a person's bloodstream, the higher the need for sexual fulfillment. Since men, on average, have a much higher level of testosterone than women, it's no surprise that they usually report a higher need. If the reverse were true—women on average having more testosterone than men—women would tend to have a higher need for sexual fulfillment.

As a rule, when men are about nineteen, they have the highest level of testosterone and lose about 1 percent a year from then on.

So again it should be no surprise that men are much more sexually motivated when they're young. Young men almost always rank sexual fulfillment as their number one need, while older men tend to give it a lower ranking.

The sexual response for both men and women can be divided into five stages: willingness and/or desire, arousal, plateau, climax, and recovery. While the stages are the same, the conditions that trigger each of them are very different for men and women. So if spouses want a mutually enjoyable sexual experience, they must communicate and accommodate these differences.

To help spouses make a successful sexual adjustment to each other, I've written forms that help improve communication and facilitate sexual problem solving. These forms begin with the *Sexual Experience Inventory*, which gives spouses an opportunity to describe their understanding of and experience with the five stages of the sexual response.

When it is difficult for a spouse to experience one or more of the five stages, I encourage him or her to complete the *Strategy to Discover the Five Stages of Sexual Experience* form. This form helps them document their plan to overcome the difficulty. After agreeing to a plan, the *Sexual Experience Worksheet* helps them document their progress.

For couples who know how to enjoy the five stages of the sexual experience but don't have sexual fulfillment in their marriage, I have written the *Sexual Fulfillment Inventory* form. This form helps spouses communicate sexual habits that they feel should be either created or avoided for fulfillment to be achieved. Another form, the *Strategy to Meet the Need of Sexual Fulfillment*, is provided to help the couple document a plan to create or avoid the sexual habits mentioned in the previous form. Finally, the *Sexual Fulfillment Worksheet* helps spouses give each other positive and negative feedback regarding their effort to create sexual fulfillment.

Forms are unappealing to many spouses. A written analysis makes sex seem too contrived for them. But my experience with couples who have actually completed the forms and then accommodated each other's sexual sensitivities and preferences has proven to me that they are very effective, and there's almost no reasonable alternative. Not only do the forms provide valuable information for goal setting, but they also hold spouses accountable for the rest of their lives together. Often spouses I've counseled refer to them years later as a reminder of what it takes for them to experience sexual fulfillment.

I've found that the primary cause of sexual incompatibility is a couple's failure to solve problems they have with the first stage of the sexual experience, willingness or desire. While testosterone puts most men in a perpetual state of willingness, and often desire as well, women don't normally feel the same way. Most women want an emotional connection before they are willing to "make love." Typically, when a woman feels bonded to a man because he's meeting her emotional needs for affection, conversation, and honesty and openness, she is willing to bond physically with him. So when a wife is reluctant to meet her husband's need for sexual fulfillment, I focus attention on his skill in meeting some of her emotional needs.

In chapter 7 I'll explain how mutual need fulfillment makes it easier for couples to meet each other's important emotional needs. Then, in part 3 of this book, I'll describe a case study of a wife who overcame her sexual reluctance when her husband overcame the Love Buster disrespectful judgments and then met her need for affection.

Disrespectful judgments are a very common cause of a wife's reluctance to meet her husband's need for sexual fulfillment. While affection causes most wives to feel emotionally bonded to their husband, disrespectful judgments block the effect of affection, making a husband's romantic gestures meaningless to his wife. So in the case study I describe, I eliminated the man's disrespectful judgments before I taught him to become an affectionate husband. If I had ignored his disrespect, his wife would not have accepted his affection.

As a rule, marriage implies sexual exclusivity. That is, a husband and wife agree to avoid sexual experiences outside of their relationship. But this agreement also implies mutual sexual availability and responsiveness. If a couple agrees to avoid extramarital sex and then one of them refuses to meet the other's need for sexual fulfillment, the agreement is very difficult to honor. For this reason, many people, particularly men, feel their spouse is obligated to make love to them. They feel entitled to have sex since they've made an exclusive commitment.

While it may sound reasonable from a legal standpoint, it doesn't hold up emotionally. As most people know, we tend to dislike doing anything we feel obligated to do. So when one spouse tells the other that he or she is entitled to have sex, it makes it inherently unpleasant for the partner. Trying to force a spouse to do anything will backfire. Instead of doing it more often, the spouse will do it less often.

Even though sex should be exclusive in marriage, it must be carefully nurtured if the need is to be fulfilled consistently. Sex should never be offered as a sacrifice and should never be demanded. The spouse with the lesser need for sex, usually the wife, should feel emotionally bonded to her husband and enjoy the experience consistently if she is to meet this need consistently. When spouses complete the forms I use to improve communication and they address the problems that the forms identify, there's rarely a complaint regarding sex.

Sex is fulfilling when it happens often enough and has high enough quality to be gratifying. But a point that bears repeating is that, unless it is mutually gratifying, sex won't be frequent enough for the one with the greater need. The more mutually gratifying it is, when both spouses look forward to a predictably enjoyable experience, the more frequent it will be.

Recreational Companionship

A need for recreational companionship combines two needs into one. First, there is the need to be engaged in recreational activities, and second, the need to have a companion. If you have a craving for recreational activities with a companion, frustrated when you don't spend enough time engaged in those activities, and fulfilled when you do, you have a need for recreational companionship. Most men rank this need high on their list of important emotional needs.

An analysis of common dating practices reflects the general tendency of most men to have this need and an effort on the part of most women to meet it. Men invite their dates to join them in attending sporting events or watching sports on TV, playing competitive games like tennis and golf, and even hunting or fishing, activities that women would rarely have chosen on their own. A woman simply wants to spend as much time as possible with the man she likes, and that means going where he wants to go.

After marriage, however, spouses tend to go their separate ways when it comes to recreational activities. He continues to watch sporting events on TV, play golf, hunt, and fish, but his wife doesn't feel that she needs to join him, since they now live together. So he does these things with male friends instead of his wife. Likewise, she shifts to recreational activities that she would have preferred even while they were dating—romantic movies on TV, concerts, theater, dining out, and the all-time favorite, shopping. Her recreational companions become like-minded women.

What's wrong with this picture? Can you see the problem? From a Love Bank perspective, she is missing a great opportunity to make Love Bank deposits. His recreational activities meet one of his most important emotional needs, and she's not around to get credit for his enjoyment.

Granted, there's something basically unfair about men expecting women to do whatever they want to do recreationally. And that's not what I propose as the solution to this problem. Instead, I encourage spouses to discover activities they both enjoy.

Consider the possibilities. There are thousands of activities a husband would enjoy if he knew they existed. And there are thousands that his spouse would enjoy. From all of these possibilities, there are hundreds of activities they would enjoy together if they knew about them. Since a couple has time to participate in about five recreational activities, you can do the math. Can they find five recreational activities that they would enjoy together just as much as those they enjoy apart?

This is how I help couples find those five recreational activities:

1. They each make a list of every recreational activity they have found or might find enjoyable. I help them get started by giving them a list of 125 common activities. (The list found in my *Recreational Enjoyment Inventory* can be downloaded free of charge from the marriagebuilders.com website.) They should also add any activities they enjoy, or think they might enjoy, that are not on my list.
2. When the couple has combined their two lists, they both rate each activity from +3 (very enjoyable) to -3 (very unpleasant). From the hundreds of possibilities, they will find that as many

as twenty or more will be given a rating of at least a +2 by both of them. These activities that they would both enjoy doing together become the focus of their recreational planning.

3. For several months I encourage a couple to limit their recreational activities to those they identified as mutually enjoyable. After trying each of them, they are to settle on five that are the most enjoyable. They won't have time for more. They document this plan on the form *Strategy to Meet the Need of Recreational Companionship* and hold themselves accountable using the form *Recreational Companionship Worksheet*.

When they get into the habit of doing the five recreational activities together, they will be each other's favorite recreational companion and will be making substantial deposits into each other's Love Bank, especially his, because this is one of his most important emotional needs.

While sexual exclusivity in marriage is a historical tradition, I encourage couples to consider recreational exclusivity as well. When a couple's favorite recreational time is spent together and not with others, particularly those of the opposite sex, not only does it help maintain Love Bank balances, but it also prevents love units from falling into the wrong accounts. I've witnessed many who have had an affair with a recreational partner because of misplaced Love Bank deposits.

Physical Attractiveness

Most men, and many women, confess that it was the physical attractiveness of their spouse that first got their attention. They may also confess that it was the primary reason they fell in love. For some people, when this emotional need is met, it can be one of their greatest sources of Love Bank deposits.

There are some who consider this need to be temporary and important only in the beginning of a relationship. After two people get to know each other better, some feel that physical attractiveness takes a backseat to deeper and more intimate needs. But that's not been my experience, nor has it been the experience of many I've counseled, particularly men. Long after a relationship has matured, love units can keep pouring into the Love Bank account of an attractive spouse, because every time he looks at her, he feels good.

When a spouse identifies physical attractiveness as an important emotional need that's not being met, I encourage the person to complete the *Physical Appearance Inventory*. This form helps the spouse communicate the changes in the appearance of the spouse that he (or she) would appreciate. The next step is for the couple to create a plan to meet the need. The *Strategy to Meet the Need of Physical Attractiveness* form is to be completed to help document the plan agreed to by the couple.

I encourage a husband (or wife) with a need for physical attractiveness to help his wife choose her clothing, hairstyle, and makeup and anything else that he thinks will affect her attractiveness. A spouse with this need is the ultimate judge of what is attractive to him, but this doesn't mean he has the right to dictate how she looks. As with sexual fulfillment and recreational companionship, these choices must be made with mutual agreement. If any emotional need is met reluctantly, it will not become a habit. Instead of being repeated almost effortlessly, it will become a constant struggle.

Ninety percent of the complaints I've heard regarding physical attractiveness are about excess weight. If spouses would simply maintain a healthy diet and exercise to avoid gaining weight from year to year, most of them would remain physically attractive to each other throughout their lives. So when the need for physical attractiveness is not being met in marriage, a weight loss plan is almost always part of the answer. While these programs abound in our society, success depends on the creation of new eating and exercising habits for overweight spouses. And the creation of these habits almost always requires accountability.

Carefully planned meals and exercise routines must be established, and weight must be reported at least weekly to a weight-loss coach (not the spouse) to hold the weight loser accountable. If a loss of more than twenty pounds is required, a physician should be consulted to monitor the weight loser's health. I encourage spouses to exercise together and to share healthy eating habits. The entire family should support the one trying to lose weight so that fattening foods are not easily accessible. Eating out should be completely avoided for most people on a diet since that's where they tend to lose ground.

I've counseled scores of women who, with a healthy diet and exercise program, along with accountability, have lost more than one hundred pounds within a year, and have kept it off for more than five years. Anyone who follows a similar plan can do it.

One question that occurs to most men who feel their need for physical attractiveness is not being met is *How do I raise the issue?* Don't most women feel terribly hurt when their husband admits they've become physically unattractive?

Technically, no one likes to hear that they're missing the mark in marriage, regardless of the need that's being unmet. But physical attractiveness is so personal that it requires special sensitivity to address.

Ordinarily I begin my assessment by asking a couple to avoid sharing the results of all of the forms they complete until I've had a chance to talk to each of them individually. That way, when a problem like physical attractiveness comes up on the *Emotional Needs Questionnaire*, I help soften the blow by mixing it among all of the other nine emotional needs. I don't emphasize physical attractiveness as a primary focus of concern. Instead, it comes up in a more objective discussion about how a husband and wife can make larger Love Bank deposits.

It's been my experience that the issue of physical attractiveness, once identified, is one of the easier needs to meet in marriage. Granted, it requires sensitivity to address it initially, but once the problem is on the table, the solution is fairly straightforward.

Domestic Support

If you have a craving for someone to wash and iron your clothes, clean your house, cook your meals, and watch your children, you have a need for domestic support. When someone does these things for you, you feel very fulfilled, but when they are not done, you feel very frustrated.

The need for domestic support is a time bomb. When a couple first marries, it seems irrelevant, a throwback to more primitive times. But for many couples, this need explodes into their lives after a few years of marriage, surprising both of them.

Typically, marriage begins with a willingness of both spouses to share domestic responsibilities. Newlyweds commonly wash dishes together, make the bed together, and divide up many household tasks. At this point the husband welcomes the help he receives from his wife with the chores he's been doing alone as a bachelor, and neither of them would identify domestic support as an important emotional need. But the time bomb is ticking.

When does the need for domestic support most often explode? When the children arrive! Children create huge needs—both a greater need for income and more demanding domestic responsibilities. The previous division of labor becomes obsolete. Both spouses must take on new responsibilities. Which ones will they perform?

Years ago it was assumed that when children arrived, husbands would work to support the family, and wives would take full responsibility for domestic support. But times have changed. Now most mothers have full-time careers and don't want to be held responsible for all of the housework and child care. They want their husband to share the responsibility with them.

However, in spite of this shift in our culture, I find many men still needing domestic support. As evidence, even when their wives work full-time, they provide very little help around the house. They do only about 20 percent of the work—not close to the 50 percent that seems fair to most women. Wives end up exhausted with overwhelming responsibilities, while husbands fall asleep in their recliners watching TV. They don't see the problem because they want their wife to meet their need for domestic support.

As a rule, most women resist my approach to this problem when they first hear it. But as is the case with other aspects of my program, when it's followed, it goes a long way toward solving a very difficult problem in marriage.

I begin by asking a couple to identify the problem. They make a list of all their child care and domestic responsibilities on a form, *Household Responsibilities Inventory*, where they name the tasks and provide a brief description. I ask each of them to rate each task from 0 to 5, with 0 indicating the task is unimportant and 5 indicating it is most important to achieve.

The next step is for each spouse to choose the tasks that he or she wants to assume responsibility for and write them on *His*

Household Responsibilities and *Her Household Responsibilities* forms. This leaves them with three lists: his responsibilities, her responsibilities, and the ones left on the original list—no one's responsibilities.

It's this third list that gets couples into trouble because the tasks need to be done by someone, but neither spouse wants to do them. So we take a look at the ratings that the spouses gave each task. I suggest assigning each task to the spouse who gave it the higher rating.

Most women howl when they hear this part of my plan, because they know that child care and household responsibilities are more important to most women than they are to most men. They end up having a list that is very long and very unfair. But at the very least, it also encourages women to see the problem for what it is—how can she expect her husband to share in household responsibilities he considers unnecessary?

At this point, a counselor is faced with an apparent contradiction. If domestic support is an important emotional need for men, why wouldn't they consider the completion of the tasks to be important? The answer is that, while men typically enjoy living in a well-managed home, they don't enjoy keeping it that way themselves. Their need for domestic support doesn't motivate them to do housework.

When it comes to getting husbands to help out around the house, motivation is the biggest problem. If a husband is asked to do something that he doesn't feel is important, how can his wife expect him to do it? Besides, if he has a need for domestic support, he'd be frustrated when his wife was not cooking and cleaning. If he had to do it himself, he'd be even more frustrated.

So when a wife looks at her list of household responsibilities, I first encourage her to eliminate as many as possible. She can hire people to do some of them, and others can be left undone.

The next part of my plan addresses the issue of a husband's motivation. I ask each spouse to rate the tasks on what's left of their lists of household responsibilities according to how much they would appreciate help for that task. The rating scale is from 0 to 5 with 0 indicating no pleasure receiving help and 5 indicating greatest pleasure with eternal gratitude. Also I ask them to indicate with an H or C if they want help (H) or want their spouse to do the task completely (C). This approach maintains the original list of responsibilities, which is admittedly unfair, but it provides an incentive for a husband and wife to help each other.

A husband may not consider a task important enough to do until he discovers that his wife needs help with it and would greatly appreciate his help. He's willing to help his wife clean up the kitchen and wash and dry the dishes after dinner if he knows it will make massive Love Bank deposits.

Therefore the final step of my plan is for each spouse (mostly the husband) to provide help where it makes the greatest Love Bank deposits. Wherever a spouse finds a 5 on the other's list, it's a signal that when the task is done, Love Bank deposits are assured. Of course the spouse's reaction to the help should determine if it is to continue into the future. If the help doesn't seem to be appreciated that much, I encourage the helping spouse to choose another task with a rating of 5.

This plan's main achievement is to create a division of labor that maximizes motivation for each spouse. It also helps couples with dual careers take a realistic look at the domestic tasks they think they need to perform. And then it addresses the need for domestic support. Technically, if a husband's need is greater than a wife's need, he will appreciate the tasks she completes, even if they're on her list. She will be making Love Bank deposits by doing what she feels needs to be done. But it has the added advantage of giving her husband extra motivation to help her with some of the tasks, causing him to make deposits into her Love Bank, even if her need for domestic support is not as great as his.

Admiration

If admiration is an important emotional need, a person is very frustrated when he or she is not respected, valued, and appreciated for what the person does and who the person is. And criticism is terribly upsetting to this person. On the other hand, when this person is complimented, he or she glows with satisfaction. A woman who once worked for me told me that my compliments

61

meant more to her than her paycheck. She had an emotional need for admiration.

But my research has proven consistently over the years that it's men who tend to have a greater need for admiration than women. In fact one of the reasons most men fall in love is that their partners give them accolades. And these women avoid making critical remarks because they know how much it hurts someone with a need for admiration.

We all have a need to be respected, valued, and appreciated, especially by the one we love. We want to be affirmed clearly and often. But there are some, especially men, whose need is so great that they will fall in love with the person who values them the most. Each time they are complimented, so many Love Bank deposits are made that it doesn't take long before their romantic love threshold is breached. So if a wife wants her husband to stay in love with her, admiration should be maximized and criticism minimized.

But often wives do the opposite. They tend to criticize their husband and rarely express their admiration. Granted, there are many valid reasons for their criticism. Their husbands may be failing to meet their important emotional needs. They may be making decisions that ignore their interests. They may be very disrespectful in the way they talk to their wife. Whatever the reason that prompts wives to be critical instead of admiring, it has a profound effect. It results in Love Bank withdrawals instead of deposits.

I show wives that they can express a complaint without being critical. The difference is in avoiding disrespect, which I will cover in chapter 8. A wife has a perfect right to tell her husband that he has made her feel bad. After all, when he's making Love Bank withdrawals, he should know about it. But she can communicate negative feedback without being critical. It's important for every spouse to know how to do that for each other, but it's crucial when a spouse has a need for admiration.

My plan to help spouses become more admiring begins by having them complete the *Admiration Inventory*. This form helps them identify behavior that either creates or destroys their admiration. Then I use the form *Strategy to Meet the Need of Admiration* to document a couple's plan to create admirable behavior and avoid behavior that destroys admiration. Finally, a couple completes the

Admiration Worksheet to provide feedback as to how the spouse needing admiration is doing.

Some wives have trouble finding value in their husbands, even though technically it's possible to find value in everyone, even their husbands. Whenever I encourage a critical wife to think of a characteristic of her husband that she admires, it doesn't take long before she can think of one and then two and then three. Sometimes wives get into a habit of being critical when with just a little effort they could get into the habit of being admiring.

After a wife thinks of a few things she admires about her husband, I encourage her to mention at least three a day. At first, it seems awkward, particularly when he knows what she's trying to do. But eventually she learns to express her admiration with conviction, and he accepts it as sincere because she really means what she says.

The Irresistible Wife

I began this chapter with the question, What is the fastest and easiest way for a woman to win a man's heart? The answer is for her to meet his five most important emotional needs.

An irresistible wife meets her husband's need for sexual fulfillment by being a terrific sex partner. She studies her own sexual response to recognize and understand what brings out the best in her; then she shares that information with him, and together they learn to have a sexual relationship that has the frequency and quality that he needs and is enjoyable for her.

She develops an interest in the recreational activities he enjoys most and tries to become proficient in them. If she finds that she cannot enjoy them, she encourages him to consider other activities that he would also enjoy. She becomes his favorite recreational companion, and he spends his most enjoyable moments of relaxation with her.

She keeps herself physically fit with diet and exercise and wears her hair, makeup, and clothes in a way that he finds attractive and tasteful. He is attracted to her in private and proud of her in public.

She manages the home and care of the children, but neither she nor he feels overworked or pressured to perform unwanted tasks.

She appreciates him more than anyone else, reminds him regularly of his value to her, and avoids criticizing him. She is proud of him and has a profound respect for the man she chose to marry.

When a woman meets these five emotional needs for a man, she deposits enough love units to breach the romantic love threshold in his Love Bank. He finds her irresistible.

6

Love Bank Deposits for Women

W omen fall in love with men the same way as men fall in love with women: Love Bank deposits breach their romantic love threshold. But the fastest and easiest ways to make Love Bank deposits are not the same for men and women.

When I asked spouses to rank ten emotional needs commonly met in marriage, men tended to rank one set of five highest, and women tended to rank the other set highest. What they were telling me was that meeting five of them would win a man's heart, and meeting the other five would win a woman's heart.

Granted, for any particular couple, there may be some crossover. The couple may identify one or two needs among their top five that are usually more important to the opposite sex. But average ratings for men and women have proven to me that what causes most men to fall in love is very different from what causes most women to fall in love.

In this chapter I'll describe the five emotional needs rated highest on average by women and the methods I use to help their husbands meet those needs. When a man meets these five needs, he becomes irresistible to a woman. As I mentioned in the last chapter, the forms I describe in this chapter are found in the workbook *Five Steps to Romantic Love*.

Affection

Some people crave affection. They like to be hugged, kissed, given cards and gifts, and told that they're loved. They're frustrated when they don't receive affection and feel very fulfilled when they do. Most of these people are women.

Affection symbolizes security, protection, comfort, and care— vitally important ingredients in any marital relationship. Affectionate acts communicate:

"I'll care for you and protect you."
"You're important to me."
"I'm concerned about the problems you face."
"I'll help you overcome those problems."

A simple hug can say these things. When we hug our friends and relatives, we are expressing our care for them. And there are other ways to show our affection. A greeting card, an "I love you" note, a bouquet of flowers, walks after dinner holding hands, back rubs, phone calls, and conversations with thoughtful and loving expressions all communicate affection.

But some people, especially husbands who do not have a great need for affection, tell me they're not the affectionate type. They explain that affection was not practiced in their family and that their wives should just get used to the way they are. The problems with this excuse, of course, are that anyone can learn to be affectionate and their wives will not "get used to the way they are" if the wives have a need for affection. An unaffectionate husband communicates the opposite of what affection would communicate:

"I won't care for you and protect you."
"You're not important to me."
"I'm not concerned about the problems you face."
"I won't help you overcome those problems."

By failing to be affectionate, a husband fails to make Love Bank deposits in one of the easiest ways possible. And for most women, his affection can make larger deposits than anything else he could do for her.

Some women will not put up with an unaffectionate husband. I've counseled many who have come to my office threatening to divorce their husband if he did not learn to be affectionate. My response is always the same: "Let's get started now. It's not very hard to learn and it won't take very long."

I ask the wife to make a list of affectionate behaviors she would enjoy. And then I ask her to make another list of behaviors that her husband may consider affectionate but she doesn't appreciate. She makes these lists on a form I call the *Affection Inventory*.

A plan for the husband to learn to be affectionate in ways that she enjoys is documented on another form, *Strategy to Meet the Need of Affection*. Then I hold him accountable to practice the affectionate behaviors that she needs and to practice avoiding behaviors she finds objectionable by using the *Affection Worksheet*, which documents his progress.

One wife I counseled suggested these affectionate behaviors:

Hug and kiss me every morning while we're still in bed.

Tell me that you love me while we're having breakfast.

Kiss me before you leave for work.

Call me during the day to see how I'm doing.

Call me when you're about to leave work so I know when to expect you.

Bring me flowers with a card expressing your love for me once in a while.

Kiss me when you come home from work and talk to me for a few minutes.

Help me with the dishes after dinner.

Put your arm around me or hold my hand when we're sitting together.

Hug and kiss me every night before going to sleep.

I encourage the husband to make copies of the list of affectionate behaviors his wife would appreciate and to check off each item during the day when he does it. After a few weeks, he doesn't need the list anymore—he's become an affectionate husband.

Granted, this approach to building affection may seem very contrived and unnatural at first, but for most husbands it's sincere. He really does care about his wife and must simply learn to communicate that care effectively. For whatever reason, he's never learned how to be affectionate, and this method shows him how to make massive Love Bank deposits.

Conversation

If you have a craving to talk about your daily experiences, personal feelings and problems, events of the day, and plans for the future, you have a need for conversation.

Ordinarily men and women don't have too much difficulty talking to each other during courtship. That's a time of information gathering for both partners. Both are highly motivated to discover each other's likes and dislikes, personal background, current interests and problems, and plans for the future. But after marriage, many women find that the man who before marriage would spend hours talking to her now seems to have lost all interest. Instead, he spends most of his spare time on his computer or watching TV. It's not that he can't talk—he simply doesn't have as great a need to talk as his wife.

So when a couple comes to me for counseling, the wife often expresses frustration with her husband's failure to meet her need for conversation. And that frustration translates into his missed opportunities to make Love Bank deposits. My solution to the problem is to help improve the quality and quantity of their conversation.

I begin by asking them to complete the *Friends and Enemies of Good Conversation Inventory*. It helps identify habits they should develop (friends) and those they should avoid (enemies).

Two of the friends involve content and two involve etiquette. The two content friends are:

1. Investigate (ask questions) and inform (answer questions) to help understand each other.

2. Develop interest in and knowledge of each other's favorite topics of conversation.

In other words, marital conversation should focus on each other and topics that interest each other.

The two etiquette friends are:

1. Balance the conversation (each should talk about the same amount of time).
2. Give each other undivided attention (look at each other while conversing).

These friends help create an enjoyable atmosphere, which in turn helps make Love Bank deposits.

The four enemies of good conversation can make a conversation so unpleasant that they cause Love Bank withdrawals instead of deposits. They are:

1. Making demands (trying to force your spouse to do something).
2. Being disrespectful (trying to minimize the value of your spouse's opinions or feelings).
3. Expressing anger (using conversation to punish your spouse).
4. Dwelling on your spouse's mistakes, past or present.

These common enemies make Love Bank withdrawals when a couple should be trying to make deposits.

After a couple identifies habits to learn and habits to avoid in their conversation, I ask them to complete the *Strategy to Meet the Need of Conversation* form to document the plan that will achieve their objective. The plan I usually recommend is to practice the four friends and avoid the four enemies of good conversation during a scheduled conversation that lasts a minimum of thirty minutes a day. The *Friends and Enemies of Good Conversation Worksheet* documents a couple's progress and helps me hold them accountable.

By taking time every day to practice using the friends of good conversation and avoiding the enemies, any spouse can learn to meet the need of conversation. And while a couple is achieving this important objective, they also learn how to resolve conflicts the right way—by showing interest in each other's perspective with respect and understanding.

Honesty and Openness

The need for honesty and openness is a craving for transparency in a relationship, with both partners revealing positive and negative feelings, events of the past, daily activities and schedules, and plans for the future.

But honesty and openness are more than a need in marriage—they are also essential for effective conflict resolution. Without honesty and openness, spouses are likely to misunderstand each other. When they lie to each other, there's little hope for finding mutually acceptable solutions to problems.

And if these reasons to be honest in marriage were not enough, there's a third reason. Dishonesty is a huge Love Buster. Even little white lies in marriage can completely undermine trust, leading to the creation of emotional barriers. Once those barriers are raised, the distrusting spouse won't allow other needs to be met, and the Love Bank drains dry.

I'll discuss the second reason to be honest (helps create effective conflict resolution) and the third reason (helps build trust) later in this book, but for now I want to focus attention exclusively on openness and honesty as an emotional need. When husbands are transparent, most wives experience a flood of Love Bank deposits. So I've created a rule for couples to follow that helps remind them that honesty is essential in marriage. I call it the Policy of Radical Honesty: *Reveal to your spouse as much information as you know—your thoughts, feelings, habits, likes, dislikes, personal history, daily activities, and plans for the future.*

> **Policy of Radical Honesty:** Reveal to your spouse as much information as you know—your thoughts, feelings, habits, likes, dislikes, personal history, daily activities, and plans for the future.

Complete honesty and openness in marriage shouldn't be considered radical, but we live in a culture where a certain amount of dishonesty is generally tolerated. Many marriage counselors, and even clergy, advise spouses to keep damaging facts, such as instances of infidelity, to themselves. They argue that to confess having an affair is cruel, especially when it was in the past.

However, I've found that when these mistakes are finally discovered, and they frequently are, it's often the dishonesty and not the mistake that does the most damage to the marriage. Confession of a mistake can be tolerated much easier than its discovery. And when a spouse knows he or she will always confess his or her own mistake, it tends to keep spouses out of trouble. They adopt necessary precautions to avoid mistakes that they know they'll later reveal.

The approach I've used to train a spouse to meet the need for honesty and openness begins with an analysis of how and why dishonesty has established itself in the marriage. By asking spouses to complete the *Dishonesty Inventory*, I help couples investigate the effect and nature of dishonesty in their marriage, each spouse's effort to control it, and each one's willingness to become radically honest.

Following that somewhat superficial investigation, I repeat it with a deeper analysis of each aspect of honesty as described in the Policy of Radical Honesty. In other words, I try to discover if a spouse may have more difficulty being honest with, say, events of the past than events of the present.

I also investigate the primary motives for dishonesty. I group most motives into four categories:

1. avoid-trouble liar
2. protector liar
3. trying-to-look-good liar
4. born liar

By analyzing dishonesty into its content and the spouse's motive, I'm able to help a couple create a plan for practicing radical honesty when a spouse might be tempted to be dishonest. That plan is documented in the *Strategy to Overcome Dishonesty* form.

After the plan is created, I ask both spouses to evaluate progress. They document their progress on the *Dishonesty Worksheet*. When spouses are being held accountable to meet most other important emotional needs, the evaluation is usually completed only by the spouse having the emotional need. But in the case of honesty and openness, the spouse who needs to be more honest and open may be more aware of instances of his or her dishonesty than the spouse having the need. So I ask them both to complete the worksheet.

Another tool that I've found to be helpful in creating a more honest and open marital relationship is my *Personal History Questionnaire* (PHQ). It's included in the marital assessment that I recommended in chapter 3. I created and used this questionnaire in the network of mental health clinics I once managed. It helped me and my colleagues gain a quick understanding of a client's personal background as part of the psychological assessment we provided in the beginning of therapy.

After having used the PHQ for a number of years, I found that often, after reading a client's responses, I knew more about the person's history than his or her spouse knew. So I began encouraging both spouses to complete the questionnaire, and with their permission, reading each other's responses. Not only did it give them both a much better understanding of each other's personal history, but it also helped trigger discussion concerning each other's thoughts and feelings.

I've found that very few therapists have been trained in teaching spouses to be honest and open. This may be due to our ambivalence regarding the value of honesty, but if you approach this emotional need as you would any habit and emphasize practicing honesty with accountability, you can train even the most private spouses to become radically honest within a few months.

Financial Support

Women marry, in most cases, for the financial security their husbands provide. But most don't fully understand or even admit to having this need until it is not being met, particularly after children arrive. I see this confusion arise when I compare the results of emotional needs surveys given to newlyweds and those given to couples who have children. New wives rarely rank financial support among their top five emotional needs, while those with children almost always include it.

One way I help engaged women understand their need for financial support is to ask the question, would you marry your fiancé if he expressed an unwillingness to earn a living? Most men, when asked that question about their fiancée, would go ahead with the wedding, but most women would not.

Emotional needs are not necessarily rational. From ancient times up to as recently as fifty years ago, a woman's need for financial support made sense. But today, with one-third of all working-women earning more than their husbands and the number steadily increasing, families don't require a husband's financial support as much. Yet, when an emotional need is met, rational or not, love units are deposited. So if a husband wants to make Love Bank deposits, he should not ignore his wife's emotional need for financial support.

My approach to teaching husbands to meet this need for their wives is based on the assumption that the need itself may be somewhat irrational, but I start with the rational part. Is he earning a reasonable income? Sometimes a simple request for a raise is all it takes to bring income up to a level that his wife believes is needed. But many men I've counseled are unemployed or underemployed. When that's the case, I direct them to vocational counseling and training that will help them get a job or improve their income.

When a man is earning a reasonable income and his wife is still unhappy about the support he provides, irrational forces may be at work. In this case, I have found that the *Financial Support Inventory: Needs and Wants Budget* can help.

First, the wife is asked to complete what I've called a "needs budget" on this form. The family's most basic living expenses, from her perspective, are calculated and totaled. If the total is less than or equal to her husband's income, then, by definition, her need for financial support has been met all along; she simply didn't recognize that his income was supporting her. In most cases, this realization solves the problem—her need for financial support is being met.

If, however, his income is reasonably adequate yet less than what she considers enough for basic living expenses, I've sometimes been able to convince her that some household expenses can be reduced so his income meets her definition of financial support. If they can't pay the bills every month, she feels that he's letting her down. But if they cut their budget and meet their household expenses with his income, in many cases she feels supported financially.

While the needs budget is the primary focus, the form includes two other budgets that a couple is to complete. First, the "wants budget" reflects the cost of meeting reasonable desires that are not considered necessities. Second, the "affordable budget" is a listing of all items from the needs budget, and some of the items from the wants that her and her husband's income can cover. In this final affordable budget, her income is designated to pay for family wants while his income pays for needs. The decisions regarding items in this final budget are made jointly.

With the Love Bank in mind, all financial decisions in marriage should lead to deposits in both spouses' accounts. Even though the wife may have the greater need for financial support, the need should be met in a way that makes the husband happy too. So a husband should avoid a career and working conditions that make him unhappy. While the support of a family is important, it should be provided in a way that grants him personal satisfaction—he should look forward to his job. *Mutual enjoyment should be the rule for meeting all emotional needs.*

> *Mutual enjoyment should be the rule for meeting all emotional needs.*

Another point that's often missed in a couple's financial planning is that a career should not prevent them from meeting each other's important emotional needs. Careers that separate spouses are particularly dangerous and are associated with high levels of divorce and infidelity. That's partly due to the fact that separation prevents spouses from meeting many of each other's most important emotional needs. The top two emotional needs for most men, sexual fulfillment and recreational companionship, and the top two emotional needs for most women, affection and conversation, are neglected when couples are separated while trying to meet a need that is not as important—financial support.

Long working hours can have the same detrimental effect on a marriage as does separation. Spouses who overwork come home exhausted and are often unable to find the energy that it takes to be a romantic partner. So when guiding a couple in career choices, make sure that the career supports the spouses' ability to meet each other's most important emotional needs. All the money in the world does not compensate for the time that a couple must spend together to be in love. I'll discuss this further in the next chapter.

Family Commitment

The emotional need for family commitment is a craving for help with the moral and educational development of one's children. When this help is provided to most mothers, Love Bank deposits are inevitable.

Family commitment is not child care—feeding, clothing, or watching over children to keep them safe. Child care falls under the category of Domestic Support that was discussed in the last chapter. Family commitment, on the other hand, is taking responsibility for the development of the children—teaching them values that will help them become successful adults. It may include reading to them, taking them on educational outings, helping them with homework, and developing skills in appropriate child-training methods.

I've found that this need cannot be met in a husband's spare time. Unless he schedules what I call "quality family time," he's likely to leave his wife frustrated. So when a wife identifies this need, I suggest creating a schedule that will bring the entire family together for the purpose of creating cooperation, respect, trust, honesty, and other important moral values.

Some of the activities I recommend for quality family time are meals together as a family, walks and bike rides, attending religious services together, family meetings, playing cooperative games, reading to the children before bedtime, helping children with their homework, and family projects. As valuable as these activities are to the children, in the context of marriage counseling their primary purpose is to meet the wife's emotional need for family commitment. So they must all be done with her enthusiastic approval. Of course, the husband and the children should enjoy them too.

I begin training a husband to meet his wife's need for family commitment by asking her to complete the *Family Commitment Inventory*. It helps her identify the type of family participation she would appreciate the most. This could include activities and skills she wants her husband to develop but also those she wants him to avoid. Additionally, she indicates how much time she would like him to set aside for these activities. In most cases, it turns out to be about fifteen hours of quality family time each week.

Next, the couple completes the *Strategy to Meet the Need of Family Commitment*, which helps them settle on a list of family activities that are mutually acceptable. The form sets them in motion by helping them schedule each week's activities and hold each other accountable for implementing the plan. The *Family Commitment Worksheet* lists the planned activities of the week and provides space to write in the activities actually done, thus showing how well the plan was followed. Both husband and wife give separate estimates of the time spent, but her estimate is the one that is to be used as the final estimate (because she's the one who has the need for family commitment). This number is entered into the *Quality Family Time Graph*, which helps them document the time their family spends together. The couple is to post the graph in a conspicuous place, such as the refrigerator door, for the entire family to see.

When a husband meets his wife's need for family commitment, not only does he help increase her love for him, but he also helps ensure the successful future of his children. He and his wife have taken the time to determine the values their children should be taught and have created effective ways to teach these values. Instead of peers being the primary source of a child's values, the parents provide them, but it can only happen with careful planning and scheduling of time.

The Irresistible Husband

What's the fastest and easiest way for a husband to win his wife's heart? The answer is for him to meet her five most important emotional needs.

An irresistible husband tells his wife that he loves her with words, cards, flowers, gifts, and common courtesies. He hugs and kisses her many times a day, creating an environment of affection that clearly and repeatedly expresses his care for her.

He sets aside time every day to talk with her. They talk about each other and about other topics that interest both of them. She enjoys the conversation because he is never demanding, judgmental, angry, or dwelling on her mistakes.

He tells her everything he knows about himself, leaving nothing out that might later surprise her. He describes his positive and negative reactions, events and experiences of the past, his daily schedule, and plans for the future. He doesn't leave her with a false impression. She can trust him to be completely truthful to her.

He assumes the responsibility to house, feed, and clothe their family. If his income is insufficient to provide essential support, he resolves the problem by upgrading his skills to improve his salary or finding a higher paying job with the skills he already possesses. He does not work long hours, keeping himself from his wife and family, but is able to support his family within a normal workweek. While he encourages his wife to pursue a career if she chooses to do so, he does not depend on her salary for essential family living expenses.

He commits sufficient time and energy to the moral and educational development of their children. He reads to them, takes them on educational outings, helps them with homework, and develops skill in appropriate child-training methods. He discusses training objectives and methods with his wife and does not apply any of these without her enthusiastic agreement.

When a husband meets these five emotional needs for his wife, he deposits enough love units to breach the romantic love threshold in her Love Bank. She finds him irresistible.

7

The Policy of Undivided Attention

Until now I've maintained that the quickest and most effective way for a couple to make Love Bank deposits is to meet each other's most important emotional needs, but now I will refine that statement and tell you the very best way to do it. It's to be in a romantic relationship with each other. I define a romantic relationship as *two people in love with each other who are meeting each other's intimate emotional needs*. This definition requires an understanding of its two crucial parts—being in love with each other and *intimate* emotional needs.

We've already discussed what *being in love* means. It's a feeling of incredible attraction to someone. It occurs when that person's Love Bank account has breached the romantic love threshold. But we have yet to discuss *intimate emotional needs*.

> *A Romantic Relationship:* Two people in love with each other who are meeting each other's intimate emotional needs.

In the last two chapters, I introduced the ten most important emotional needs. Five of them were ranked highest by most men, and the other five were ranked highest by most women. While all five are important, only two of the five from each list are intimate emotional needs, because they are the most personal and the most commonly met when I observe spouses in dating relationships (a romantic relationship prior to marriage) and while having an affair (a romantic relationship outside of marriage).

The four intimate emotional needs are affection, conversation, recreational companionship, and sexual fulfillment. When a couple considers their relationship to be romantic, these four emotional needs are usually being met.

> **The Four Intimate Emotional Needs:** affection, conversation, recreational companionship, and sexual fulfillment.

One might argue that honesty and openness and physical attractiveness are also intimate needs. I don't deny that they are important ways to make Love Bank deposits. However, many if not most affairs are based on pervasive dishonesty, yet they thrive when the four needs I've mentioned are being met. And I've also found, in most cases, a lover is not nearly as physically attractive as the spouse. Intimacy, it appears, is blind for most people.

So when I try to help a couple restore their love for each other, in spite of what they report in the *Emotional Needs Questionnaire*, I focus most of my attention on the four intimate emotional needs. When met, they make the largest Love Bank deposits. But they don't affect men and women equally. Two tend to be the intimate needs of men—sexual fulfillment and recreational companionship—and two tend to be the intimate needs of women—affection and conversation. When all four of these needs are met on a date, both husband and wife consider it to be a romantic experience and the best way to make large Love Bank deposits.

When a couple is dating, they try to meet each other's needs for intimacy, and so all four emotional needs are usually met. But after marriage, they try to take shortcuts. A husband wants his wife to have sex with him and join him in his favorite recreational activities without having to be as conversant and affectionate as he used to be. A wife wants her husband to talk to her and express his love for her regularly, but is often reluctant to make love or join him in recreation, as she did before marriage. In other words, they want their own needs met as in the past but are not as willing to meet their spouse's needs.

Over time, their reluctance to meet each other's intimate emotional needs erodes their Love Bank balances, and they find themselves out of love with each other. When this happens, they often feel awkward trying to meet each other's intimate emotional needs. It just doesn't seem natural when you're not in love anymore.

It's the negative feedback loop I mentioned earlier. A negative response of one spouse triggers a negative response in the other. Less conversation and affection by the husband makes the wife feel less willing to make love or watch football with him. Less lovemaking and recreational companionship from the wife leads to even less conversation and affection by him. The downward spiral continues until there is little or no affection, conversation, recreational companionship, or sexual fulfillment. When these needs are not being met, the feeling of love evaporates and a romantic relationship ceases to exist.

Most of the couples I've counseled had already lost their feeling of love for each other when I first saw them. Their Love Bank balances were not only below the romantic love threshold, they were often below zero. They were in the red!

> *A Negative Feedback Loop:* A negative response of one spouse triggers the negative response of the other.

So what was the quickest way to restore their love for each other? Somehow I had to encourage them to start meeting the intimate emotional needs that helped create the love they had when they said, "I do."

That's a tough assignment when you are facing a couple who doesn't love each other anymore. And it seems impossible when they hate each other. Yet I've found that if I can do it, their love is always restored. I have yet to witness a single failure when I've been able to motivate a couple to meet these four emotional needs for each other.

I'm sure you can imagine how many couples have tried to talk me out of my plan to restore their marriage by their meeting each other's intimate emotional needs. And their primary argument is that they don't have time to rekindle their relationship. They're too busy doing things that are far more important. But it doesn't take much insight to recognize how a couple's love for each other is the most important aspect of their relationship. It's even more important than their careers or care for their children because these priorities can be destroyed by a loveless marriage. On the other hand, when a couple is in love, their careers are more successful and the care of their children more effective. A great marriage supports everything else that's important to a couple.

As we go back to my definition of a romantic relationship, remember that it consists of two parts: two people in love (part 1) who meet each other's emotional needs for intimacy (part 2). Since meeting the needs for intimacy is the quickest and most effective way to restore love, it makes sense to begin with that goal when counseling a couple. Once a couple actually meets those needs for each other, it's only a matter of time before enough Love Bank deposits are made to trigger romantic love. When this happens, meeting intimate emotional needs becomes almost effortless, making ever-increasing Love Bank deposits. This is the reason I say that the *very* quickest and most effective way for a couple to make Love Bank deposits is to be in a romantic relationship.

> *A great marriage supports everything else that's important to a couple.*

The Policy of Undivided Attention

I have created a rule that helps guide a couple toward a romantic relationship by encouraging them to meet each other's four intimate emotional needs. It's the Policy of Undivided Attention: *Give your spouse your undivided attention a minimum of fifteen hours each week, using the time to meet his or her need for affection, sexual fulfillment, conversation, and recreational companionship.*

There are three aspects of this policy that require expansion and clarification: privacy, objectives, and time. Let me explain each of these to you one at a time.

> *Policy of Undivided Attention:* Give your spouse your undivided attention a minimum of fifteen hours each week, using the time to meet his or her need for affection, sexual fulfillment, conversation, and recreational companionship.

Privacy

A couple should establish privacy so they are able to give each other undivided attention. The time they plan to be together should not include children (who are awake), relatives, or friends.

Intimate emotional needs can be met only when undivided attention is given. Affection is most intimate when a couple is alone. Conversation is intimate when others are not present. Recreational companionship is the same. It's not really meeting an intimate emotional need when others are with you, unless you're lost in a crowd. And it goes without saying that sexual fulfillment requires privacy. Without privacy, undivided attention is almost impossible. And undivided attention is an essential ingredient for intimacy.

One of the most important lessons I teach new parents is how to be together without the baby present. It's a very difficult lesson to learn, especially for women. And yet, without privacy, intimate emotional needs cannot be met; and when they are not met, romantic love is lost.

There are many books written about how couples will inevitably lose romantic love, especially after children arrive. The authors argue that it's unrealistic to assume that the passion of early love can be sustained. But that hasn't been my experience, nor has it been the experience of thousands of other couples who maintain privacy after children arrive.

When a husband and wife are together with their children, they can meet another important emotional need, family commitment. And as I mentioned in the last chapter, this need should be met, not only for the sake of the wife, but also for the sake of the children who need two involved parents. But family commitment is not an intimate emotional need and it will not make large enough Love Bank deposits to compensate for unmet intimate emotional needs. It's only when family commitment is met along with intimate emotional needs that marriage finds its greatest fulfillment.

Friends and relatives can be a threat to a romantic relationship, especially when a family is large. Often spouses are tempted to sacrifice time with each other so they don't neglect family members or lifelong friends. My advice to these couples is to take care of each other's intimate needs first and then make time for friends and relatives.

Cell phones are another unwanted distraction when a couple is trying to create privacy. As a rule, I recommend leaving them home or use them only in emergencies while on a date.

How "undivided" must attention be? Would seeing a movie together count toward your time for undivided attention? It would if you behave like the couple sitting in front of my wife and me last week. I don't think they really saw the movie. It's the same with television and sporting events. If you're being affectionate while watching an event together and giving each other your attention, it counts. Otherwise, it doesn't.

Objectives

During the time a couple is together, they should create activities that will meet all four of the intimate emotional needs of affection, sexual fulfillment, conversation, and recreational companionship. As I mentioned earlier, after marriage, a woman often tries to get her husband to meet her emotional needs for conversation and affection, without meeting her husband's needs for sexual fulfillment and recreational companionship. On the other hand, a man wants his wife to meet his needs for sexual fulfillment and recreational companionship, without meeting her needs for affection and conversation.

Neither strategy works very well. Frequently, women resent having sex without affection and conversation first, and men resent talking and being affectionate with no hope for sex. By combining the fulfillment of all four needs into a single event, however, both spouses have their needs met and enjoy the entire time together.

A man should never assume that just because he's in bed with his wife, sex is there for the taking regardless of how the evening was spent. If he has not devoted time to his wife, she will probably feel ambushed and very resentful. But an evening of undivided attention, with affection and conversation, leads very naturally to a very enthusiastic sexual ending. If a woman's emotional needs are met, there's no resentment in meeting her spouse's emotional needs.

When the intimate emotional needs are met in appropriate ways, the largest Love Bank deposits are made. The time devoted to undivided attention each week turns out to be the most enjoyable time of the week for a couple, especially when they're finally in love with each other. But it may not begin that way. At first, because they are not in love, they may find that trying to meet each other's intimate emotional needs is very awkward, boring, or even unpleasant. This is particularly true when a couple has not learned to meet each other's needs appropriately. Conversation can be argumentative instead of caring, affection can be artificial instead of from the heart, recreational activities can be enjoyable for only one spouse, and sex can be downright scary.

As spouses learn to meet each of these needs with sensitivity and skill, however, the awkwardness turns into anticipation. When this happens, it isn't long before they're in love, and they value their time for undivided attention above all else.

Time

The number of hours a couple schedules to be together each week for undivided attention should reflect the quality of their marriage. If the marriage is satisfying to both spouses, they should schedule fifteen hours each week to be together. But if they suffer marital dissatisfaction, they should plan more time until marital satisfaction is achieved.

How much time is needed to sustain the feeling of love? In my investigation of dating patterns of college students that lead to marriage, it became clear to me that at least fifteen hours of undivided attention was a crucial factor. When couples were too busy to invest that amount of time in each other, the relationship usually fell apart. On the other hand, when they spent even more time with each other, the marriage was often moved up.

I applied this discovery to married couples and found that if I could motivate them to give each other at least fifteen hours of undivided attention, their love for each other would be restored. By spending even more time together, they fell in love faster.

When I apply the fifteen-hour rule to marriages, I typically recommend that the time be spent in three- to four-hour blocks. This way, all four intimate emotional needs can be met whenever undivided attention is given. Quite frankly, it's the way most college students who ended up married dated each other.

Of course, a couple should also meet intimate emotional needs spontaneously. Talking to each other and being affectionate whenever there's an opportunity are marks of a couple in love. But there's no substitute for planning when it comes to romance. The word *date* draws us to the importance of scheduling time for undivided attention. If it were not scheduled prior to marriage, most couples would never have made it down the aisle. If it's not scheduled after marriage, the love that brought the couple together quickly evaporates.

It isn't easy to motivate couples to take time for undivided attention. One problem I've already mentioned is that it's more difficult for them to meet each other's intimate emotional needs when they're not in love. It feels awkward being affectionate and making love when the spark just isn't there. So they come up with excuses to avoid the dates they've scheduled. Their children must be driven to soccer practice; a special project must be completed at work; they're not feeling well enough to go out. I've heard them all, but the bottom line is that they don't really want to meet each other's intimate emotional needs.

I've already discussed the value of coaching. It's requiring someone to do what he or she doesn't want to do so the person can be what he or she wants to be. That's the way I approach the problem of undivided attention. I require a couple to spend a minimum of fifteen hours together each week so they can be in love with each other.

If couples don't schedule time for undivided attention when they feel disconnected and out of love with each other, they won't have an opportunity to learn how to make their time together enjoyable. By waiting weeks, months, or even years hoping that somehow their relationship will recover, they waste precious time. Instead of enduring an unpleasant and unfulfilling marriage, they could have been enjoying each other with passion and romance.

At first, the time spent together sometimes seems like a total waste. But as the couple learns how to meet each other's needs effectively, it becomes increasingly enjoyable for both of them. The fifteen hours of undivided attention is like a blank canvas. What a couple does with the time is the painting. As they become skilled in meeting the needs of affection, conversation, recreational companionship, and sexual fulfillment, it becomes the most enjoyable time of the week—a time that neither would ever want to miss. Then the canvas becomes a masterpiece.

Learning to Schedule Time for Undivided Attention

It takes time to meet intimate emotional needs, and the only way time can be found in most couples' busy lives is to schedule it. Without a schedule, it simply doesn't take place. So I use a formal approach to help couples create the schedule.

I encourage spouses to meet each other at 3:30 every Sunday afternoon to plan their time for undivided attention. They look over each other's schedule for the coming week and block out the time they need. I encourage them to schedule a little extra time for undivided attention just in case a planned date must be moved due to an emergency.

I provide a *Time for Undivided Attention Worksheet* to help a couple keep a record of what was planned and how the time was actually spent. It also gives each spouse an opportunity to judge how much time was given to undivided attention. The amount of time entered on the worksheet is the amount estimated by the spouse who indicates the lower amount—generally the wife. A couple uses the worksheet from the prior week to help plan the following week's activities. Each week they try to make their time together more enjoyable and intimate.

Another form, the *Time for Undivided Attention Graph*, provides a record of how many hours a couple actually spends meeting intimate emotional needs. The lower estimate given by either the husband or wife is the one that's recorded on this graph. I encourage a couple to post the graph in a prominent place, like the refrigerator door (where there may already be a *Quality Family Time Graph*), so their children can see if they are achieving their goal. The graph helps children understand the reason their parents need privacy, and it also teaches them what they will need to do some day to keep love in their marriage.

When I see a couple for the first time, I let them know that my program will require a minimum of fifteen hours a week of their time. If they can't dedicate that much time while I'm counseling them, I suggest they find another counselor because my plan won't work without it.

At first, they spend most of the fifteen hours completing the lessons I assign, practicing new skills. But when the counseling is over, and their marriage is secure, they are to continue scheduling the fifteen hours of undivided attention for the rest of their lives together.

Meeting important emotional needs is only half of the story, however. While that's how couples make the most Love Bank deposits, they must be sure that they're not depositing into a sieve. They must also avoid making Love Bank *withdrawals*.

The next three chapters introduce the common ways that married couples hurt each other. You'd think that causing pain and suffering would be the last thing a married couple would want to do to each other, and yet it's done instinctively and habitually. Unless a couple protects each other from their destructive instincts and habits, they will hurt each other so much that eventually their Love Bank accounts will be drained dry—and even drop into the red.

By the time many of the couples make their first appointment with me, their Love Banks are so bankrupt that they hate each other. This is because they have unleashed an arsenal of weapons that make each other miserable. So I must not only teach them to make Love Bank deposits but also how to stop making withdrawals.

8

Control and Abuse

Love Bank balances have a tremendous effect on human behavior. When someone has a large balance in his or her account in our Love Bank, our emotions encourage us to keep the person around. We are armed by our emotions with thoughtful and generous instincts and want to reciprocate by making deposits into the person's Love Bank.

But when someone has a negative Love Bank balance, our emotions do the opposite. They discourage us from doing anything that would make the person part of our lives. Instead of being thoughtful and generous, our instincts encourage us to be thoughtless and cruel. We do what we can to put a "leave me alone" sign on our door.

In most of our relationships, people don't have much opportunity to make large Love Bank withdrawals, because we drive them away from us before they can do much damage. But in marriage, because of a commitment to stay together "for better or worse," Love Bank withdrawals can continue unabated. Eventually a thoughtless spouse will trigger the "hate" response.

Consider the possibilities. Sam innocently annoys Karen while, at the same time, failing to meet her intimate emotional needs of affection and conversation due to pressures at work. As a result Sam's account in Karen's Love Bank falls below zero. Karen's instinctive reaction is to stop meeting Sam's intimate emotional needs of sexual fulfillment and recreational companionship and to start being disrespectful and angry, causing her account in his Love Bank to fall below zero.

As the couple's Love Bank accounts drop from just below zero to far below zero, their destructive behavior escalates. What had been a relationship of mutual care now turns into a relationship of mutual harm. Eventually their emotions win the day by convincing both of them that the sooner they divorce, the better. End of story.

Throughout my counseling career, I've been aware of the dark side in all of us. I've seen it in almost everyone. We have the ability to override our destructive instincts, but it takes a great deal of effort to achieve that objective, particularly when someone has hurt us.

Love Busters

I have a name for habits that make Love Bank withdrawals. I call them Love Busters because that's what they do. They destroy the feeling of romantic love.

During the marital assessment, one of the forms I ask couples to complete is the *Love Busters Questionnaire*. It helps them identify the ways they make each other unhappy, causing large withdrawals from each other's Love Bank. One of my goals is to teach them how to avoid this mistake. There's no point in learning how to make Love Bank deposits if Love Bank withdrawals abound.

> **Love Busters:** Habits that make Love Bank withdrawals and destroy the feeling of romantic love.

Based on the results of the *Love Busters Questionnaire*, I focus a couple's attention on their thoughtless *habits*—behaviors that are repeated—because they do the most damage in marriage. Isolated instances of thoughtlessness can damage Love Bank accounts, but when thoughtlessness occurs again and again, becoming a habit, it has devastating consequences. And as most psychologists know, almost all of our behavior is in the form of habits. We tend to repeat ourselves.

But habits can change. They're formed when we do something many times and they can be modified when we do something else often enough. You learned to type on a traditional keyboard by practicing until it became almost second nature to you. You have developed the habit of typing. You're hardly aware of your keystrokes as you type a report. But what if keyboards were to change? What would you do if the letters were in different places? By practicing with the new keyboard, you could become just as proficient with the new as you had been with the old.

Any habit can change by practicing a new, overriding behavior. So if one habit makes Love Bank withdrawals, it's possible to replace it with a new habit that makes deposits. Even instinctive behavior can be modified by learning new habits.

I've found that all habits that cause Love Bank withdrawals fall into six categories. Three are habits of control and abuse—selfish demands, disrespectful judgments, and angry outbursts. The other three create incompatibility—dishonesty, annoying behavior, and independent behavior.

This chapter will describe the first three Love Busters and the way I teach couples to overcome them.

Thoughtless Problem Solving Strategies

Conflicts abound in marriages. Joyce and I have at least one each hour we're together and yet we have a great marriage. That's because we resolve our conflicts in a caring and thoughtful way. We consider each other's feelings and interests whenever we have a problem to solve.

High Love Bank balances tend to make thoughtful resolutions to conflicts instinctive. And since Joyce and I have been in love throughout our forty-six years of marriage, we rarely even feel like being thoughtless toward each other. But that's not the case for most couples who seek help for their marriage. They are usually not in love, and often their typical problem solving strategy proves it. When they have a conflict, instead of considering each other's feelings, they ignore each other's feelings. Either they try to force their will on each other or they withdraw from each other and solve the problem independently.

I'll discuss the second strategy when I introduce independent behavior in chapter 10. In this chapter I'll focus on the first strategy, when a couple tries to force their will on each other. I like to call this the "dictator strategy." It assumes that in marriage a spouse should be able to control the other spouse. And when control fails, he or she has a right to be abusive.

Logically, control and abuse in marriage make little sense. It's supposed to be a relationship of extraordinary care, not extraordinary harm. Besides, control and abuse don't get the job done. They don't resolve conflicts. The only clear effect of control and abuse in marriage is that Love Bank withdrawals are made. Why would spouses deliberately hurt each other in an effort to get what they need when it doesn't work?

Viewing control and abuse from an instinctive perspective makes more sense. When Love Bank balances are negative, spouses no longer feel like caring for each other. Instead, they feel like hurting each other. They don't want to be loved when their Love Bank accounts are in the red—they want each other out of their life.

Of course, there are those who seem to want their spouse around, even though they're being controlling and abusive. They will even accompany their spouse to marriage counseling sessions. But if you understand the psychological dynamics of these people at the time that they're being abusive and listen closely to what they're actually saying during an angry outburst, it's clear in most cases that they really want to sweep their spouse out the door.

So with the dictator strategy in mind, I'll introduce you to the first three Love Busters: selfish demands, disrespectful judgments, and angry outbursts. They're the controlling and abusive ways that couples try to resolve marital conflicts, usually when they've lost their love for each other.

As a reminder, all of the forms I mention are found in *Five Steps to Romantic Love*.

Selfish Demands

I consider marriage to be a partnership of equals. A husband and wife should have equal rights, and no decision should be made unless they are in agreement (I'll discuss this concept in more detail in chapter 10). There should be no sergeants and privates in marriage, only five-star generals.

My egalitarian approach to marriage is based partly on the fact that mutual Love Bank deposits cannot be made unless both spouses consider each other's feelings in everything they do. Unless both spouses resolve conflicts thoughtfully, one spouse's gain risks being the other spouse's loss. My goal for the couples I counsel is for them to make Love Bank deposits simultaneously. Neither should gain love units at the expense of the other's account.

Control in marriage does the opposite. Instead of making simultaneous Love Bank deposits, control can cause simultaneous withdrawals. And it begins with a demand—one spouse commands the other to do something.

In many marriages, particularly after romance has ended, this form of problem solving is the rule. Negotiation seems out of the question. There is one option only—try to force the other person to do what is needed by demanding it. A demand is a misguided way to solve a problem by trying to force a spouse to accept a solution. It's controlling because it gives a spouse no right to refuse. It's abusive because refusal implies subsequent punishment. "If you don't do what I demand, you'll soon wish you had." But threats don't work well in marriage. They're not motivating. In fact demands with implied threats are more likely to create resistance than cooperation. If you want your spouse to stop doing something for you, start demanding it.

The wiser alternative to a selfish demand is a thoughtful request. It begins with the question, "How would you feel if you were to help me by . . . ?" It's a *request* because the other spouse can refuse without abusive consequences. It's *thoughtful* because it expresses concern for the other spouse's interests. And it's *motivating* because it carries with it a request for help—a way to make a Love Bank deposit.

> **A Demand:** A misguided way to solve a problem by trying to force a spouse to accept a solution.

To help couples identify, and then eliminate, selfish demands from their marriage, I first ask them to complete the *Selfish Demands Inventory*. It's designed to identify the effect and nature of selfish demands, each spouse's effort to control such demands, and each one's willingness to stop making them. The inventory gives a couple an opportunity to reflect on their own selfish demands as well as those made by their spouse.

In this phase, I encourage the couple to understand their instinct to hurt each other and how demands have not solved their problems. I want them to consider an alternative that demonstrates their care for each other—one that works.

The hard part comes after identifying selfish demands—changing the behavior. I recommend to couples that they replace their habit of selfish demands with the habit of thoughtful requests, and that requires practice. The form *Strategy to Replace Selfish Demands with Thoughtful Requests* helps them document their plan. By using the question I've recommended—How would you feel if you were to help me by . . . ?—they have opportunity for daily practice. The guidelines I recommend to a couple are described on pages 63–68 in *Love Busters*.

Two more forms, *Selfish Demands Worksheet* and *Thoughtful Requests Worksheet* are designed to help the couple document their successes and failures to eliminate this Love Buster. I review these worksheets with them during their appointment.

Granted, there are rare situations when demands may be necessary in marriage. During a spouse's affair, for example, I recommend that the betrayed spouse demand that there be no contact with the lover. If there is continued contact, separation or even divorce would be the logical consequence. While normally demands don't work, in this case there are no reasonable alternatives because thoughtful requests are even less likely to separate lovers.

Disrespectful Judgments

Respect is an essential ingredient to effective problem solving in marriage. That's because each spouse must incorporate the other's perspective if a mutually acceptable solution is to be found. I'll develop this concept further in chapter 10, but for now I'll simply make the obvious point that without mutual respect, marital conflicts are rarely resolved.

Not only is disrespect in marriage ineffective, it's controlling and abusive—controlling because a spouse uses it to try to impose his or her way of thinking on the other; abusive because it hurts a spouse by ridiculing and devaluing his or her opposing views.

Selfish demands are sometimes rationalized by claiming that the task demanded is somehow good for the other spouse or that the demand is simply a reminder of responsibility. Disrespectful judgments are often rationalized in the same way—the criticism is in the spouse's best interest. But the true reason for disrespectful judgments is to force a spouse to adopt a certain attitude, belief, or behavior that's in the demanding spouse's best interest. And it's usually not in the best interest of the other spouse.

While a selfish demand is the first stage of abuse and control in marriage, a disrespectful judgment is the second stage. Ordinarily it's used when demands don't work. And since demands rarely work, disrespect follows in most cases.

When a demand to carry out the garbage isn't obeyed, it doesn't take long before laziness and irresponsibility are mentioned. The judgment can be muttered just loud enough to be heard or yelled out so that everyone in the house is notified.

It may seem obvious to us that such a comment is a disrespectful judgment, but the one being disrespectful is sometimes unaware of this. For many people the habit of disrespect is so entrenched that it may even seem respectful to the one making the judgment. So I recommend that each spouse ask the other a series of questions to determine if this Love Buster has invaded their marriage. The questions are as follows:

Do I ever try to "straighten you out"?

Do I ever lecture you instead of respectfully discussing issues?

Do I seem to feel that my opinion is superior to yours?

When we discuss an issue, do I interrupt you or talk so much that you are prevented from having a chance to explain your position?

Are you afraid to discuss your point of view with me?

Do I ever ridicule your attitudes, beliefs, or behavior?

In case there's any question as to whether a comment is a disrespectful judgment, the spouse who feels disrespected is to be the judge. There's nothing wrong with one spouse trying to influence the other with an honest exchange of ideas, but when the conversation turns into one forcing an opinion on the other, it's disrespectful.

The wise alternative to disrespectful judgments is respectful persuasion, which requires spouses to discuss the conflict with respect rather than argue about it with disrespect.

I use essentially the same approach to eliminate disrespectful judgments as I use to eliminate selfish demands. I begin with the *Disrespectful Judgments Inventory* to help a couple identify the effect of disrespectful judgments on each other, their nature, each spouse's effort to control them, and each one's willingness to eliminate them.

As with the habit of selfish demands, I encourage spouses to replace disrespectful judgments with another habit that gets the job done. I teach them to create the habit of respectful persuasion to be used whenever they disagree about an opinion, belief, or behavior. With respectful persuasion, a spouse tries to win the other over in ways that are safe, pleasant, and respectful, and both spouses acknowledge the value of each other's opinion. The form *Strategy to Replace Disrespectful Judgments with Respectful Persuasion* helps document the plan they agree to follow. The general plan I recommend is described on pages 79–84 in *Love Busters*.

To learn the habit of respectful persuasion, couples must practice using it daily until it becomes second nature. Two more forms, the *Disrespectful Judgments Worksheet* and *Respectful Persuasion Worksheet*, help a couple document their successes and failures. I hold them accountable by reviewing these forms with them during their appointment with me.

Angry Outbursts

The third and most dangerous stage of control and abuse is angry outbursts. When demands and disrespectful judgments don't produce the desired outcome, an angry outburst is often unleashed as a final effort at gaining control and as a punishment for failure to submit. An angry outburst has no place in marriage, or anywhere else for that matter, for a wide variety of reasons. But the most important reason is that it causes massive Love Bank withdrawals. It's one of the most effective ways to lose a spouse's love.

Angry outbursts are examples of temporary insanity. People who are having a temper tantrum are capable of almost anything, including murder. And that's an extremely important fact for a counselor to acknowledge when faced with violence in marriage. When someone is having an angry outburst, people's lives are at risk. When a counselor knows that a spouse is in a violent relationship, he or she should do everything possible to protect that person, suggesting separation with a restraining order, if necessary.

Granted, we're born with an instinct to have angry outbursts and we demonstrate it convincingly the moment we leave the womb. We enter the world angry. But while our capacity for anger is there for good reason at the time of our birth, as adults, it can get us into all kinds of trouble. So most of us learn to overcome angry outbursts by dealing with frustration calmly and intelligently. Those who do not learn this lesson run the risk of losing their job, their friends—and their spouse.

As with selfish demands and disrespectful judgments, I encourage spouses to have zero tolerance for angry outbursts. When angry spouses try to defend their behavior by blaming each other, I quickly explain that no one makes us controlling and abusive. Demands, disrespect, and anger are behaviors that all of us can completely eliminate if we choose to do so. In fact my approach to helping a spouse overcome angry outbursts begins with him or her acknowledging personal responsibility for their behavior. Unless a spouse knows that he or she is 100 percent responsible for their angry outbursts, any program of anger management is doomed to failure.

Early in my life, I had a very bad temper and, like most angry people, I blamed others for my outbursts. But one day as I was having a very frustrating experience trying to replace the transmission in my car, I had an insight that would change my life. In my frustration, I blamed the car for my failure to install the new transmission and went to work beating on it with a hammer. When I had finally calmed down, I realized that for a moment I'd been insane. The car wasn't being uncooperative. It was entirely my fault. And yet in a fit of rage, I wanted to punish the car.

From that time on I recognized that when I had an angry outburst, I was paranoid and irrational. When I allowed myself to lose my temper, I was not an emotionally healthy person. So I went to work training myself to avoid angry outbursts at all costs.

When faced with frustrating circumstances, I learned to relax instead of become increasingly agitated. When I had finally cooled off, I would approach the problem with a plan that had a high probability of success. Over time, with practice, I didn't even feel angry when frustrated. The neural pathways in my brain had changed so that frustration no longer led to anger, but instead led to attempts to solve the problem rationally.

This plan for overcoming angry outbursts is described on pages 97–113 in *Love Busters*. The entire chapter on angry outbursts is well worth reading, because I explain in more detail how foolish and dangerous angry outbursts are in marriage and how important it is for everyone to eliminate them entirely.

Overcoming Control and Abuse

Since selfish demands, disrespectful judgments, and angry outbursts can blend into each other, it's sometimes difficult to tell them apart. And frequently they appear in a cascading manner, escalating so fast that they seem to come all at once. So generally, I treat them all as a single problem—control and abuse.

Once a spouse rejects the assumption that he or she has the right to tell the other spouse what to think or do and that his or her angry outbursts are never someone else's fault, I can help the person create new habits that replace the controlling and abusive habits. The new thoughtful habits make successful negotiation possible.

I want each spouse to be fulfilled in marriage. I want their needs to be met. But control and abuse do the opposite. These habits prevent spouses from meeting each other's needs. They lead to a very unfulfilling and dangerous marriage, because they combine into a problem solving strategy that doesn't work. Instead of leading a couple to marital fulfillment, they lead them to marital disaster.

But these habits are instinctive, and that's the reason they're so difficult to address in marriage counseling. Just as meeting intimate emotional needs is instinctive when Love Bank balances are above the romantic love threshold, control and abuse are instinctive when Love Bank balances are negative. If a couple is to overcome these Love Busters, they must do what they don't feel like doing. They must ask for help when they feel like demanding it. They must learn to be respectful when they don't feel an ounce of respect toward each other. They must learn to relax when they feel like flying into a rage. And it's your job as a counselor to help them do what they don't feel like doing so they can become what they want to be.

9

Dishonesty and Annoying Behavior

The three Love Busters we just discussed—demands, disrespect, and anger—all have something in common. They are controlling and abusive attempts to solve a marital problem. The next Love Busters—dishonesty, annoying behavior, and independent behavior (in chapter 10)—also have something in common. They have a devastating effect on marital compatibility.

If a spouse is dishonest, any attempt at trying to create a compatible lifestyle will be thwarted. Disinformation leads spouses to shoot at targets that don't exist and miss the real targets completely. If annoying behavior is left unchecked, a spouse's habits, however innocent, will make him or her very difficult to tolerate. And if spouses engage in independent behavior, they create lifestyles that are very inhospitable to each other.

Dishonesty

When we discussed the emotional need for honesty and openness, I introduced the Policy of Radical Honesty: *Reveal to your spouse as much information as you know—your thoughts, feelings, habits, likes, dislikes, personal history, daily activities, and plans for the future.* It's a marital rule that helps spouses, especially husbands, make large Love Bank deposits.

When emotional needs are not being met, some Love Bank withdrawals are inevitably made because of the frustration spouses feel when their needs are neglected. But the failure to meet the needs for honesty and openness not only makes a few withdrawals due to frustration, but it also makes massive withdrawals when a spouse is dishonest. For that reason alone, spouses should make the Policy of Radical Honesty their lifelong commitment to each other.

Counselors are sometimes confused about this Love Buster. Deep down, they know that spouses should be honest, but how far should it go? Should a spouse be honest when the truth is so painful that it can cause a divorce? When a wife first learns, ten years after it happened, that her husband was unfaithful while she was pregnant with their first child, it's so painful that she sometimes wishes she had been left ignorant. When a husband discovers that his wife had an affair with his best friend while he was deployed overseas in the military, it's like a knife in his back. So if the affair is over, should it be revealed?

That's a question most counselors hear from time to time from unfaithful spouses who want to be truthful yet are afraid that the truth will ruin their marriage. It's sad that many, if not most, counselors recommend dishonesty. I've heard some argue that it's thoughtless to reveal a past indiscretion. The only purpose for this, they suggest, is to help lift the feeling of guilt from the unfaithful spouse. The emotional relief gained by telling the truth heaps pain and misery onto the betrayed spouse. They recommend a more thoughtful plan—keep the betrayed spouse in the dark and learn to endure the guilt.

My position on this topic is to be honest at all costs, and it has been consistent throughout my professional life. The reason I call my rule of honesty "radical" is that there should be almost no exceptions, even when it comes to infidelity. At first, I made this recommendation based on the moral assumption that honesty trumps marital survival. But as I witnessed the application of the rule in marriages that suffered from infidelity, I came to the conclusion that radical honesty actually saves marriage. The truth makes it easier, not more difficult, for couples to create a fulfilling marriage, even when a spouse has had an affair.

You may have caught the word *almost* in the last paragraph. I wrote that there should be "almost no exceptions." What exceptions do I allow? I have always told couples that, if following the rule of honesty puts either of them in mortal danger, it should not be followed. For example, if an insane wife is holding her family hostage, threatening to kill them all, her husband should tell her anything to avoid disaster. When a wife is trying to escape from a physically abusive husband, she has the right to lie about her plans until her escape is complete. In these cases, the dishonesty helps prevent physical harm.

If a wife is afraid to admit an affair to her husband because of his history of physical violence, I suggest that she first separate and then reveal it from a safe distance. But in the vast majority of cases I've witnessed, honesty has not triggered a violent reaction. Instead, it's when dishonesty is eventually discovered that the unfaithful spouse is at greatest risk of physical violence.

Another exception to radical honesty is disrespectful judgments. If you think your spouse is being lazy or stupid, should you tell your spouse your thoughts? Is it dishonest to keep disrespectful opinions to yourself? I encourage spouses to have zero tolerance for disrespectful judgments. Under no circumstances should a couple say anything disrespectful to each other. While it's impossible to avoid occasional disrespectful thoughts or opinions, they should not be spoken.

For example, if Joyce asks me if a certain outfit she's chosen to wear makes her look fat, I give her my honest opinion. Some outfits do and some don't. But I wouldn't tell her that an outfit makes her look unattractive unless she asked me or if I already knew that she would value my critical judgment. However, if an outfit she wants to wear makes me feel uncomfortable for some reason, I should reveal that fact, even when she hasn't asked for my opinion.

An unsolicited, "You look fat in that outfit," is disrespectful. But, "That outfit bothers me," is a respectful way to express an honest emotional reaction. If she wants to know why it bothers me, I can go on to say that it doesn't flatter her figure as much as other outfits do. If she persists in knowing the basis for my remark, I can then admit that it makes her look fat.

Some counselors suggest that a husband should always be admiring, even if it's dishonest, but I have always been honest in the way

I admire Joyce. That way she always knows that my accolades are from the heart. She would far rather have an honest husband with a little less admiration than a dishonest one with fabricated praise.

What I've said about disrespectful judgments also goes for selfish demands and angry outbursts. I've had more than one spouse tell me that when they're being demanding and angry, they're merely expressing honest feelings. But selfish demands and angry outbursts are not really pure feelings at all—they are feelings that have been contaminated with control and abuse. There are ways to express feelings honestly without being demanding, disrespectful, or angry.

When we discussed honesty and openness as an emotional need in chapter 6, my strategy for helping a spouse meet this need focused on breaking habits of dishonesty and replacing them with habits of honesty. I use the same forms and basic strategy for couples who identify dishonesty as a problem in their marriage, so I won't repeat them again in this section. But in almost all cases, when a spouse identifies honesty and openness as needs that are being neglected, the Love Buster dishonesty is also identified as a problem to be solved.

Annoying Habits

Annoying habits are repeated behaviors that unintentionally cause a spouse to be unhappy. They include personal mannerisms, such as the way people eat, clean up after themselves (or don't!), snore, drive, and talk.

While almost all of us find our spouse to be annoying occasionally, it's generally wives who are the most annoyed. I've come to this conclusion after reading thousands of *Annoying Habits Inventory* forms that I've asked couples to complete. This form asks each spouse to list habits of the other they find annoying, and it contains space for five annoying habits, but more than one copy of the form can be used. For almost every couple I've counseled, the wife's list has been far longer than the husband's list. In one case the wife typed out twenty-four single-spaced pages that listed all of her husband's annoying habits.

The difference in the responses of husbands and wives may have something to do with the differences in the ways their brains are constructed. A female brain has far more connections between neurons than a male brain has, and the band of fibers connecting the right and left hemispheres (corpus callosum) is much thicker for women because there are many more fibers. These neurophysiological differences could be what account for a woman's greater sensitivity to her surroundings. While men may be able to ignore behavior that might otherwise be annoying, blocking it out of their consciousness, women may not be able to do this as easily. But whatever the reason, when a wife finds her husband's behavior annoying, Love Bank withdrawals are being made from his account, and the husband should take this seriously.

It's tempting for husbands (and counselors) to suggest that wives should not complain as much as they do. After all, when a wife complains about a husband's annoying behavior, doesn't that cause withdrawals to her account in his Love Bank? Wouldn't it be wise to keep her complaints to herself, thereby helping maintain his love for her?

An analogy can be made in financial banking. Suppose withdrawals are being made to your bank account that you have not authorized. And your personal banker feels that notifying you about the withdrawals may upset you, so he decides to keep it to himself. Eventually, your account is overdrawn, but again, the banker does not want to upset you with this information and, instead, bounces your checks and charges your account for each overdraft. He sends you a fictional statement each month that does not mention the unauthorized withdrawals, the bounced checks, or the overdraft charges. What will eventually happen?

The same thing can occur in marriage. If a wife does not mention withdrawals, they take place without a husband's knowledge. Eventually, these innocent, annoying habits drain so much from his Love Bank account that it's in the red. But she doesn't tell him that either. Instead, she tells him that she loves him right up to the day she files for divorce.

I've witnessed many of these cases, where wives feel that it's wrong to complain and even worse to tell their husband they've lost their love for him. By the time the wife leaves him, his Love Bank balance is so negative that the wife feels no hope in restoring her love for him.

For this reason, I've encouraged wives to complain, especially about annoying behavior. Why keep a husband in the dark when his Love Bank account is being drained? When she complains, she gives him the choice of either doing something about it so that the "unauthorized withdrawals" are stopped, or letting them continue, risking the loss of her love for him.

At this point I must add a caveat to my encouragement of wives to complain. A complaint is simply a warning that love units are being withdrawn—nothing more, nothing less. But I am very much opposed to criticism as a way of communicating a complaint. When a wife uses a disrespectful judgment to accent the complaint, it becomes a criticism, and that's a Love Buster. A complaint is, "It bothers me when you leave the glass on the counter." A criticism is, "By leaving the glass on the counter, you prove how sloppy you are," or, ". . . how little you care about me." A criticism is a disrespectful judgment, while a complaint is simply an expression of a negative emotional reaction.

My approach to helping couples, especially husbands, eliminate annoying behavior begins with the *Annoying Habits Inventory* I mentioned above. The first part helps identify the presence of annoying habits in marriage. It not only lists annoying habits but also indicates how often the habit normally occurs and how annoying each habit is to the spouse on a scale of 1–10 (1 is slight annoyance and 10 is extreme annoyance).

Typically, the list includes a few habits that can be easily overcome with a simple decision to stop doing them. In most cases, these are new habits that have not been hardwired into a spouse's brain or habits that don't provide much gratification. These habits can be checked off the list if they don't reappear after a decision to stop has been made.

The annoying habits that remain on the list are those that cannot be easily eliminated. These habits will require special planning. So I recommend that the annoyed spouse select the three most annoying habits from this list to be eliminated first.

The second part of the *Annoying Habits Inventory* focuses special attention on these three most annoying habits. By providing the background and nature of each habit, this form helps a couple create a plan. And the plan for each of the three habits is documented on the form *Strategy to Overcome Annoying Habits*.

The plan for overcoming an annoying habit is to practice an overriding, nonannoying habit under the same conditions. For example, if the annoying habit is leaving your socks on the floor after taking them off at night, the plan might be to practice putting your socks in the hamper whenever you take them off. To speed up the habit formation, you would practice putting your socks on, then taking them off and putting them in the hamper, say, ten times a day for a week. After one week's practice, if you continue to put your socks on the floor when you take them off at night, your daily practice would be extended for another week. Most people find that their new habit is formed within days, although some can take three weeks or longer.

The *Annoying Habit Worksheet* documents progress toward overcoming each of these habits. As the counselor, you would review this form during your counseling session to hold the annoying spouse accountable.

A word of warning: when spouses make a complete list of annoying habits, it can be very risky because a very long list can cause the couple to conclude that they are not right for each other. For this reason, at the beginning, I recommend that the lists be no longer than ten items. That way, as I shepherd a couple through the elimination of three annoying habits, the number remaining doesn't seem so overwhelming. Eventually they discover that what is possible for three is possible for almost any number.

10

Independent Behavior and the Policy of Joint Agreement

The most common cause of marital arguments is independent behavior. I define this sixth Love Buster as *activities that are conceived and executed by a spouse as if the other doesn't exist.* It should be no surprise that spouses argue when one ignores the interests and feelings of the other.

Those who engage in independent behavior have excuses that are often supported by popular cultural values. Marriage, they argue, should not prevent a person from trying to

> **Independent Behavior:** Activities that are conceived and executed by a spouse as if the other doesn't exist.

achieve long-held dreams; one spouse should not limit the other's potential in life; and some decisions are very personal and should be made exclusively by the individual. These and many similar arguments focus on the value of the individual's judgment and see joint agreement in marriage as being dangerously limiting.

I see it the other way around. I find joint agreement in marriage to be far wiser than anything either spouse could discover on his or her own. In general, joint decisions are wiser than individual decisions because they take more into account. This is particularly true when solving marital problems. Usually, the combined perspective of a man and a woman provides a broad and farsighted framework on which wise decisions can be made. It's like a man looking in one direction, and a woman looking in another. Together they take in more of the landscape than either can see.

But making unwise decisions isn't the primary reason I'm opposed to independent behavior. My main objection is that it destroys romantic love. When one spouse chooses to do something that offends the other spouse, Love Bank withdrawals result. To avoid this outcome, I recommend interdependent behavior: *activities that are conceived and executed with the interests of both spouses in mind.* This behavior recognizes that decisions in marriage should benefit and protect both spouses. Neither spouse should try to gain at the other's expense.

> **Interdependent Behavior:** Activities that are conceived and executed with the interests of both spouses in mind.

The five most common conflicts in marriage are over friends and relatives, career choices and time management, financial planning, child discipline, and sex. When decisions are made independently—that is, one spouse does what he or she pleases without considering the interests of the other—incompatibility is the final outcome. The lifestyle that these decisions create makes life pleasant for one spouse at the expense of the other.

Love Bank withdrawals also result. The independent behavior and arguments that follow drain the Love Bank. And if that were not bad enough, the conflict is not resolved, making future Love Bank withdrawals inevitable.

The only way to prevent massive Love Bank withdrawals in marriage is to resolve conflicts the right way—with the interests of both spouses taken into account. Every decision should be made jointly, which prevents an argument and solves the problem.

Compatibility in marriage depends on the way a couple makes decisions. If they make them independently of each other's feelings and interests, they'll eventually find themselves very incompatible, even if they began their relationship perfectly compatible. But the most incompatible couple can create compatibility by learning to take each other's interests and feelings into account when they make lifestyle choices.

The Policy of Joint Agreement

Using the Love Bank assumption as a guide, I've come to the compelling conclusion that win-win decisions make marriages thrive, while win-lose decisions make them fail. If decisions that make Love Bank deposits to one and withdrawals to the other can be changed to make simultaneous Love Bank deposits, marriages can succeed.

As I was developing rules that would maximize Love Bank deposits and minimize their withdrawals, I came to the realization that problem solving in marriage is a habit, and if I could train couples to become skilled in the habit of win-win negotiation, it would be much easier for them to sustain romantic love.

This approach to problem solving, to make the goal mutual agreement, turns marriage into a partnership instead of a sole proprietorship. And it gives the partners in marriage equal standing. If mutual agreement is their goal, neither spouse should have the last word or make the final decision. Until a decision can be made with mutual agreement, spouses should continue to negotiate.

I've written a rule that encapsulates this approach. I call it the Policy of Joint Agreement (POJA): *Never do anything without an enthusiastic agreement between you and your spouse.* I used the word *enthusiastic* instead of *mutual* because of the temptation most couples have to make reluctant agreements. I wanted a rule that would guarantee deposits into both Love Banks, and "enthusiastic" gets the job done.

Couples who already have an interdependent lifestyle have no trouble following the Policy of Joint Agreement. They're already doing it. Even before I became a successful marriage counselor, it's how my wife, Joyce, and I resolved all of

> **Policy of Joint Agreement:** Never do anything without an enthusiastic agreement between you and your spouse.

our conflicts. And it's how my parents and Joyce's parents resolved their conflicts.

I estimate that spouses in about 20 percent of all marriages follow this rule without ever having been introduced to it. These are the marriages that are most successful. But for the remaining 80 percent, the rule may seem ridiculous. They are accustomed to doing what they please, making independent decisions, and then fighting about them.

When I first introduce this rule to these couples, they think I'm exaggerating. *How can any couple make all decisions with enthusiastic agreement?* they wonder. Even if they finally agree that some couples do follow this rule, they don't think it's possible for them.

In practice, spouses who come to enthusiastic agreements don't spend the day asking each other how they feel about every single issue. Most decisions are made with the knowledge that, if asked, they would both agree with enthusiasm. Negotiation begins when one of them raises an objection to an activity or behavior that the other spouse has innocently planned or has already completed. The offending spouse is now on notice that the activity or behavior cannot continue in its present form. Discussion that leads to enthusiastic agreement is in order.

Conflicts are common even in the best marriages. That's because, as a rule, men and women see the world so differently. As I've stated earlier, Joyce and I have at least one conflict every hour we're together and we're together far more than the fifteen hours a week that I recommend. But in our forty-six years of marriage, we've never had an argument. That's because a conflict triggers a respectful discussion not a fight. When a conflict arises, we try to discover a win-win resolution that will make both of us happy.

What about Resentment?

One of the most common objections to the POJA is that it creates resentment when it's followed. I agree; it does usually create some resentment. But far more resentment is created when it is not followed. An illustration will help make this important point.

George is invited to watch football with his friend Sam. He tells his wife, Sue, that he plans to accept the invitation. Sue objects.

If George goes ahead and watches the game, he's guilty of independent behavior. He is not following the POJA, and Sue will be resentful. When George *does* something against the wishes of Sue, I call her resentment type A.

If George follows the POJA and doesn't accept Sam's invitation, George will be resentful. When George *is prevented from doing* something because of Sue's objections, I call his resentment type B.

Which type of resentment makes the largest Love Bank withdrawals: type A or type B? The answer is type A, and that's why the POJA helps build Love Bank balances. I'll explain.

When George violates the POJA, Sue has no choice but to feel the effect of the thoughtless decision (Love Bank withdrawals) for as long as memory persists—possibly for life whenever the event is recalled. But when George follows the POJA, the negative effect is limited in time. It lasts only as long as it takes to discover an enjoyable alternative that is acceptable to Sue.

George lets Sue know how disappointed he is with her objection but is willing to discuss other options. Sue wasn't invited to watch football and doesn't want to invite herself to Sam's house, so she suggests inviting Sam and his wife to their house to watch football. George calls Sam, he and his wife accept, and the new activity puts an end to George's type B resentment.

Type A resentment can last forever, but type B resentment stops the moment a mutually enjoyable alternative is discovered. Those with poor negotiating skills may have trouble seeing the difference because they have not learned how to resolve conflicts. They may feel resentment about a host of issues that have been unresolved in their marriage. But after you teach a couple to negotiate successfully, unresolved issues are minimized. Then it becomes clear to them that the POJA helps build Love Bank balances by eliminating type A resentment.

The Four Guidelines to Successful Negotiation

Joyce and I usually reach enthusiastic agreement very quickly when a conflict arises, and the process we follow seems almost effortless to both of us. But for someone who's unaccustomed to coming to enthusiastic agreements in marriage, the process can seem daunting, if not impossible. So I've written the *Four Guidelines to Successful Negotiation* (FGSN) to help couples learn how to reach an enthusiastic agreement when conflicts arise. The procedure I recommend can seem very contrived and uncomfortable at first, but after practicing it for a while, it becomes second nature even to couples who have been in the habit of arguing instead of negotiating.

Guideline 1: Set Ground Rules

Before a couple discusses anything, they should guarantee to each other that their conversation will be pleasant and safe. It is essential to set ground rules to accomplish this. They should convey their care for each other with smiles on their faces and protect each other by avoiding demands, disrespect, and anger at all costs. If one spouse feels that the discussion is becoming unpleasant or unsafe, they should postpone it until a later time when they've been able to regain emotional control.

Guideline 2: Try to Understand Each Other's Perspective

A couple should be respectful and listen to each other's point of view as they discuss their conflict. What is the issue and how do they both feel about it? What would each of them like? If they were to have their way, how would it affect the other person? Is there a way to have what they want with their spouse's enthusiastic agreement?

During this first phase of problem solving, radical honesty with respect is essential in understanding each other's perspective. Spouses should not judge the value of a perspective that does not agree with their own. Instead, they should try to think of ways to incorporate it into a final resolution.

One of the biggest mistakes spouses make in this phase of problem solving is trying to get their point across without showing much interest in the other spouse's position. To avoid this mistake, I encourage each spouse to be the first to ask the other how he or she feels about the issue. And I don't want them to express their own opinion until the other spouse asks for it. Each spouse already knows how he or she feels—each of them has yet to understand how the other spouse feels. And neither spouse can think creatively about a resolution until he or she fully understands both perspectives.

Sometimes it's valuable for spouses to repeat each other's position to be sure they understand it. I want them to be empathetic, imagining what it would be like to think the way the other one thinks about the issue.

I can't emphasize too much that disrespect is a poison pill when it comes to negotiating. The quickest way to end a discussion and completely eliminate all hope of coming to an enthusiastic agreement is to be critical. On the other hand, when spouses try to understand each other and accommodate each other's perspective when trying to resolve a conflict, they encourage further discussion.

Guideline 3: Brainstorm with Abandon

For many conflicts, it isn't easy to find a resolution that accommodates the perspectives of both spouses, so they will need to give their brains time to do some of the heavy lifting by letting the problem incubate.

When a conflict is first discovered, a mutually agreeable resolution may not occur to either spouse immediately. They should carry a pad of paper or PDA around with them so they can record possible solutions as they occur to them. It may take days before they have accumulated several possibilities, and they must remember that, for a resolution to be acceptable, it should accommodate both of their perspectives simultaneously.

Guideline 4: Find the Best Solution

In their effort to find a solution with which both spouses enthusiastically agree, they should daily check each other's list of possibilities until they find one that clicks. They should spend some time discussing each idea, even if it's rejected, explaining how the idea works and how it doesn't work. But they should do it respectfully.

Often I recommend a test of a possible solution if there is uncertainty. A trial period for implementing it can generally be agreed to enthusiastically as long as it's understood to be a test. If the test proves the idea to be successful, they've found a winner. If it fails, the couple should keep brainstorming.

Sometimes a couple may not be able to resolve a conflict. I know of many happy marriages where some conflicts remain unresolved for the life of the couple. When that happens, the couple simply doesn't act. The default condition of the Policy of Joint Agreement is to do nothing, and in most cases, that is not as damaging as independent behavior.

The way couples go about trying to resolve a conflict is more important to the success of a marriage than the resolution itself. They are more likely to hurt each other with an argument, or a unilateral decision, than to leave the conflict unresolved. And a conflict is not resolved the right way until both spouses agree enthusiastically.

Resolving Common Marital Conflicts

As I mentioned at the beginning of this chapter, the most common marital conflicts typically fall into one of five categories: friends and relatives, career choices and time management, financial planning, child discipline, and sex. Books have been written that single out each of these as the primary cause of divorce. But it isn't the focus of the conflict that ruins a marriage—it's independent behavior and the way couples try to address it.

The Policy of Joint Agreement puts an end to independent behavior and the Four Guidelines to Successful Negotiation puts an end to arguments. Taken together, they help create marital compatibility by changing a couple's way of life from benefiting one spouse at the expense of the other to benefiting both spouses simultaneously.

Activities involving friends and relatives should be managed to create mutual comfort. The POJA directs a couple to temporarily end a relationship that offends one spouse. Then the FGSN helps a couple find a way to reestablish that relationship or create new relationships that make both spouses happy.

Frequently, career choices and time management go hand in hand. Sometimes a spouse feels that the scheduling demands of a career should be the highest priority in marriage and should be nonnegotiable. Family schedules should yield to work schedules since it's work that pays the bills. But career requirements may interfere with the meeting of intimate emotional needs and quality family time. When I'm told that it's impossible to schedule fifteen hours a week for undivided attention and another fifteen hours a week for quality family time, I realize that the requirements of a career make it seem impossible.

The POJA and FGSN help a couple reorder their priorities. A career should help strengthen a family not weaken it. If spouses agree to follow these guidelines, a career will eventually serve the family instead of the family serving the career.

By and large, conflicts over money begin when one spouse makes a significant purchase without the other spouse's knowledge or agreement. They argue over each other's "rights" instead of making an effort to find mutual agreement through negotiation.

The POJA clears up the "rights" issue—neither spouse can spend their money without the other's enthusiastic agreement. The conflict changes from how a spouse has already spent money to how a spouse wants to spend it. After they know that enthusiastic agreement is required before making purchases, they learn what the other person will agree to without having to ask, allowing each other increasing discretion.

The right way to train children sometimes requires the wisdom of Solomon. But short of having Solomon as advisor, two heads are better than one, especially when they're the natural parents. They bring an instinctive understanding of their children to the table that can't be matched elsewhere.

I've found that when both parents agree enthusiastically on child-training objectives and methods, patience is maximized and abuse is minimized. Children tend to turn out much happier and more successful when their parents are on the same page. The POJA and FGSN help create that blending of wisdom that leads to effective parenting.

Sex is another common area of conflict in marriage, but unless it's resolved with mutual enthusiastic agreement, this very important emotional need will not be adequately met. The POJA and FGSN help create the best sex possible in marriage.

In general, whatever the couples you counsel need in marriage, whether it's friends, time, money, sex, or anything else, arguing about it with demands, disrespect, and anger is likely to get them less of it in the future. I want the couples I counsel to get everything they need—in abundance—from each other. And the way that's achieved is through thoughtful negotiation.

Granted, the POJA and FGSN are not instinctive to most couples. They are born to fight with each other instead of negotiate. But even born fighters can learn to follow the POJA and FGSN. It takes plenty of practice with lots of mistakes along the way. But when a counselor helps a couple get what they need from each other in a thoughtful way, the marriage is not only saved, but those lessons are usually passed on to children who are also genetically predisposed to argue instead of negotiate.

So far in this book, I've introduced you to the theory and method of my approach to helping couples. Now I'd like to put it all into practice by describing how I would actually counsel a couple from intake to discharge. In the next three chapters I'll try to answer many of the questions you may have at this point about application.

PART 3

APPLICATION

A Case Study

11

Intake and Assessment

The last section contained descriptions of the treatment plans I've used to help couples fall in love and stay in love with each other. But I don't want you to think that I use all of these plans for every couple. Instead, I focus on the problems that a particular couple presents and help them solve those that prevent them from being in love. In most cases, after these problems are solved and they're in love, they can solve the rest of them on their own.

I will describe the procedure I have followed when counseling couples face-to-face in an office setting. I do this because you are likely to counsel couples in the same way, primarily because third party payers require it. But in Appendix C, I offer an argument for an alternative, telephone counseling. In the future, I believe that most marriage counseling will be conducted by telephone or over the internet.

The following case study demonstrates how I might use selected treatment plans in a program that requires only ten sessions. It's a composite of several cases I've witnessed, all successful, where the presenting complaint was that the wife was not happy about meeting her husband's need for sexual fulfillment.

Making the First Appointment

A client whom I had counseled a few years earlier referred Amy to me. She called my office on Monday for information, and my appointment secretary answered her questions to her satisfaction. My first appointment with her and her husband, Jack, was scheduled for 2:00 p.m. on Thursday, three days later. They both had to miss work to make that appointment. There was another marital therapist in the clinic who could have seen them on Wednesday evening, but they preferred to counsel with me.

Occasionally a prospective client will ask to speak directly with me before making a final decision to make an appointment. In such cases, my secretary will arrange for a time that we can talk for about five minutes by telephone. If I had spoken with Amy, I would have made it clear that I could not evaluate her problem or make recommendations before talking with her and her husband, but I would have described my qualifications, experience, and rate of success with the problems she faced.

Session 1: Intake

Amy and Jack were asked to arrive at my office fifteen minutes early to complete intake forms, which included registration, insurance information, contracts, and confidentiality agreements.

At 2:00 p.m. I met them in the waiting room and asked who would like to be first to talk with me. Amy volunteered, and Jack agreed to let her go first. I talk with each spouse separately because I want to allow each of them to describe their marital problems but I don't want them to offend each other while doing it. Usually, spouses blame each other, and that can be a very unpleasant first experience with me if they are together.

With only fifteen minutes to get a rough idea of Amy's perspective, I began by asking her, "How would you like me to help you and Jack?"

"I hate having sex with Jack, but I feel guilty when I turn him down," she replied.

"Have you always felt this way?" I asked.

"Not in the beginning. I was probably more interested in sex than Jack was at first. I couldn't get enough of him. But after we had been married for a while and had two children, I lost interest. I feel something once in a while, but it's normally not when we're together."

I told her that I thought I could help her with the problem and asked if she had other marital problems.

She thought for a minute and said that ordinarily they got along okay when they were together but they were alone very seldom. Since both of them worked full-time and their two children, Jessica (8) and Ryan (6), wanted their full attention when they were home, they had little time for each other.

After that brief interview I escorted Amy back to the waiting room and Jack followed me to my office.

I asked Jack the same question I had asked Amy, "How would you like me to help you and Amy?"

Jack really didn't know what to say. Amy had told him that they would be seeing a marriage counselor and that he had to take the afternoon off from work. Quite frankly, he didn't know quite what to make of it. He was afraid that she might be having an affair with someone at work and wanted to reveal it during the session.

I assured him that an affair was not mentioned during my interview with her and I went back to asking him how I could help them.

"I suppose that we're not really having much of a marriage lately. It's go to work, take care of our kids, sleep, and then go to work again. I'm trying to be a good husband and father but apparently it's not good enough for Amy."

"Is there anything you'd like from her?" I asked.

"I'd like her to be happy," was his first reply. Then, after a short pause, "And I'd like a little sex once in a while."

"I can help you. Wait here while I ask Amy to join us."

I went to the waiting room and asked Amy to follow me back to my office. When we were together, I told them that I could help them accomplish the goals they had described to me, but first they should complete all of the forms that I handed them in two manila envelopes. Each envelope contained:

1. *Emotional Needs Questionnaire* (ENQ)
2. *Love Busters Questionnaire* (LBQ)

3. *Marital Problems Analysis* (MPA)
4. *Personal History Questionnaire* (PHQ)
5. *Marital Counseling History Questionnaire* (MCHQ)
6. *Love Bank Inventory* (LBI)

They were to complete these forms independently of each other and were not to discuss their answers. It would take about five hours to complete them all. I explained that they would be able to see most of each other's forms after the next session, which would be the assessment.

I paused for a moment and then in a serious tone of voice assured them that their problems could be solved only if they would reserve fifteen hours each week for the assignments I'd be giving them and if they would complete the assignments before each session. They both agreed to my terms, although at the time they didn't know where they'd find the fifteen hours.

I walked them to the appointment desk where they made a three-hour appointment with me for the marital assessment. It was scheduled for the following Saturday from 2:00 to 5:00 p.m.

> Throughout my career, I have counseled three evenings and Saturdays for the convenience of the couples I counsel. I give new couples prime hours (evenings and Saturdays) to make it easier for them to get the help they need. In the case of Amy and Jack, I had to make their first appointment on a weekday afternoon because all evening and Saturday hours were already taken, and they were unwilling to see another available counselor in the clinic.

Session 2: Assessment

My assessments require three hours to complete—one hour for each of the spouses meeting with me alone and a third hour to create goals that both spouses agree to achieve. Since either spouse can take the first hour, they need not come to the office together. If they want to come together, however, I tell them to bring something to do while they wait. In many cases, the spouse who completed the forms is first, while the other, who is not quite finished, spends the first hour racing through the remaining questionnaires. That was the case with Amy and Jack.

Amy's Assessment

Since Amy had decided to be first, I asked her to follow me to my office. Then immediately I began reading to myself the answers on her *Emotional Needs Questionnaire.*

I turned to the ranking of emotional needs first (on the last page of the form) and saw that she listed them as follows:

1. Affection
2. Conversation
3. Family Commitment
4. Financial Support
5. Admiration

In most cases, the need for openness and honesty is third among the top five needs for the average wife, but Amy had replaced it with the need for admiration, which she ranked fifth in importance. It's not unusual for a spouse to deviate somewhat from the average ranking—not everyone is average. It's common for a particular woman to list one or even two needs that the average man would place on his list of five important emotional needs. This is the reason I ask each husband and wife to tell me what he or she considers to be most important.

I checked the Likert scales under the A section of each page of the ENQ to make sure they were consistent with the rankings. For example,

A Likert scale is a graphic continuum used to rate the level of feeling about something. For instance, the first item on the *Emotional Needs Questionnaire* is, "Indicate how much you need affection by circling the appropriate number." Below the item are the numbers 0 (I have no need for affection) through 6 (I have a great need for affection). It can also be used to reflect the degree with which a person agrees or disagrees with a statement. That type of Likert scale is used in the *Love Bank Inventory.*

since affection was Amy's number one emotional need, the Likert scale rating would be expected to be 5 or 6 (I have a great need for affection). Since the ratings of the needs ranked 1–5 were all consistent with the rankings, I assumed that she had given the issue adequate thought and that I could be reasonably sure it was an accurate judgment.

Amy had also answered the questions under the Likert scales (if she felt happy when the need was met, and unhappy when it was not met by Jack). These answers were also consistent with someone who felt the needs she had identified.

Then I examined the scales under section B of each page on the ENQ where Amy was asked how satisfied she was with Jack's meeting those five needs. Amy had given a 3 rating (extremely satisfied) for Family Commitment, 2 for Financial Support, and 1 for both Admiration and Conversation. But Affection rated a -3 (extremely unsatisfied). In other words, Jack was not meeting Amy's top need, Affection.

The most effective way for Jack to make deposits into his account in Amy's Love Bank was being ignored. That being the case, I would assume that she was no longer in love with him. But the final verdict would be determined later in the hour.

Next I read Amy's answers to the LBQ. Her rankings of Love Busters were as follows:

1. Disrespectful Judgments
2. Angry Outbursts
3. Annoying Habits
4. Selfish Demands
5. Dishonesty
6. Independent Behavior

Once again I compared the Likert scale ratings at the top of each page of the LBQ with the rankings and they were consistent. In other words, Disrespectful Judgments was given the highest rating (6—I experience extreme unhappiness), and Independent Behavior was given the lowest (3—I experience moderate unhappiness).

The next item on each page asks how often Jack made any of these mistakes. I discovered that the category of Disrespectful Judgments was a huge problem for Amy. Not only was it the mistake that made her most unhappy, but it was made several times every day, according to her accounting.

The remaining Love Busters were made so infrequently that they didn't affect her Love Bank very much. Amy couldn't remember the last time Jack had an angry outburst, the second highest rated category.

My tentative hypothesis based on the ENQ and the LBQ was that Jack was failing to make large Love Bank deposits by ignoring Amy's emotional needs for affection, and he was making massive Love Bank withdrawals by being disrespectful several times a day. The result was likely turning out to be a negative Love Bank balance. I expected the MPA, the next form for me to review, to confirm my tentative hypothesis.

The first part of the MPA asks a spouse to respond to each of the ten emotional needs and six Love Busters with one of the following:

1. Serious enough to threaten our marriage unless resolved
2. Serious but not enough to threaten our marriage if left unresolved
3. Sometimes disappointing but not a serious problem
4. No problem at all

Amy gave none of the sixteen categories a rating of 1 but gave a 2 rating to Affection and Disrespectful Judgments. Now I was confident as to what I would be encouraging Jack to do for Amy, and what he should avoid doing to her.

Typically, the PHQ and MCHQ take me about five to ten minutes to read. Since sexual fulfillment was one of Amy's presenting problems, I paid special attention to the "Sexual History" part of the PHQ. She reported no history of sexual abuse, and her sexual experiences seemed normal.

The MCHQ indicated that she had not read a book, attended a seminar, or visited a counselor for marital problems. That made my job easier, since many popular approaches to marital therapy conflict with mine.

Finally, I scored her *Love Bank Inventory* (see appendix A). It takes only a few minutes to score because there are only 20 items to be added. The total score, adding positive ratings and subtracting negative ratings, was 6. Dividing that number by 20 gave me a quotient of 0.3. That number was barely positive, which indicated that Amy liked Jack a little but she was not close to being in love because it did not reach my estimate for romantic love of 1.8. Her answer to question 21, "I am in love with Jack," was 0, supporting my conclusion.

Amy was not in love, but she didn't dislike Jack, either. This fact gave me confidence that I could help them overcome their problems within ten sessions. If her Love Bank balance had been negative, it would probably have taken me longer than ten sessions to motivate her to cooperate with her part of the plan.

On three copies (one for each spouse and one for my own records) of the form *Memorandum of Agreement* (see appendix B), I filled in the date and Amy's and Jack's names at the top of the first page. On the second page that lists emotional needs the husband agrees to meet, I entered Affection, Conversation, Family Commitment, Financial Support, and Admiration on lines 1 through 5. I put an asterisk before "Affection," since Jack had not been meeting that emotional need.

Then on page 3 where it lists Love Busters that the husband agrees to avoid, I entered, Disrespectful Judgments, Angry Outbursts, Annoying Habits, Selfish Demands, Dishonesty, and Independent Behavior on lines 1 through 6. I put an asterisk before "Disrespectful Judgments" as a reminder that Jack had to learn to avoid that Love Buster.

During this one-hour assessment with Amy, I had come to the tentative conclusion that Jack's failure to meet her emotional need for affection and his failure to avoid making disrespectful judgments were the primary causes of her lack of love for him. He was making a few Love Bank deposits in meeting her needs for conversation, family commitment, financial support, and admiration, but they were all being withdrawn by his disrespectful judgments. Tentatively I assumed that her lack of romantic love for him was one reason she found it difficult to meet his need for sexual fulfillment. The other reason was that affection is a primary environmental condition for most women. Without affection, Amy would rarely be in the mood for sex.

After briefly discussing my conclusions with Amy, she agreed that they were correct. I escorted her to the waiting room and asked Jack to follow me to my office.

Jack's Assessment

On the last page of the ENQ, Jack's listing of his top five emotional needs were as follows:

1. Sexual Fulfillment
2. Physical Attractiveness
3. Recreational Companionship
4. Family Commitment
5. Admiration

As with Amy's list, Jack's list also included one need that was more characteristic of the opposite sex—Family Commitment. It had taken the place of the average husband's emotional need for domestic support.

The Likert scales in the A sections of Jack's ENQ were consistent with the rankings. The responses under the Likert scales (if he felt happy when the need was met and unhappy when it was not met by Amy) were also consistent with someone who felt those needs.

When I reviewed the second part of each page on the ENQ, which asked how satisfied Jack was with Amy's meeting of these five needs, a 3 rating (extremely satisfied) was given for Physical Attractiveness, 2 for Family Commitment, and 1 for Admiration. But Recreational Companionship rated a -2 and Sexual Fulfillment a -3 (extremely unsatisfied). Amy was not meeting Jack's number one and number three emotional needs.

Amy was making Love Bank deposits because she was very attractive, and that was fulfilling Jack's second most important emotional need. But her failure to meet his needs for sexual fulfillment and recreational companionship left him feeling very frustrated.

I discussed these conclusions with Jack, and he agreed that they accurately described his feelings.

Then I reviewed Jack's answers to the LBQ. His rankings of Love Busters were as follows:

1. Selfish Demands
2. Angry Outbursts
3. Independent Behavior

4. Annoying Habits
5. Dishonesty
6. Disrespectful Judgments

A comparison of the Likert scale ratings on the top of each page of the LBQ with the rankings was consistent.

The question on each page asking how often Amy made these mistakes revealed that none of them had been a problem for Jack. As with all Love Busters, when someone does them, we don't like it. And Jack felt the same way. But Amy had protected Jack from these destructive habits, and they rarely affected him.

The results of the ENQ and the LBQ led me to the conclusion that Amy was making Love Bank deposits by simply looking attractive, but she could be making many more deposits if she were to meet Jack's emotional needs for sexual fulfillment and recreational companionship. Since she was not making significant withdrawals, I suspected that her account might be high enough for him to be in love with her.

The next form I reviewed, the MPA, would provide further evidence to either support or refute my conclusions. Repeating what I said earlier, the first part asks a spouse to respond to each of the ten emotional needs and six Love Busters with one of the following:

1. Serious enough to threaten our marriage unless resolved
2. Serious but not enough to threaten our marriage if left unresolved
3. Sometimes disappointing but not a serious problem
4. No problem at all

Jack rated none of the sixteen categories with a 1 and only one category, Sexual Fulfillment, was rated a 2. His need for recreational companionship, apparently, was not that important to him, since he rated it a 3.

I discussed recreational companionship briefly with Jack. He told me that with so many responsibilities, they really didn't have time for them. But he felt that it was something they both missed since their children had arrived. At present they work to pay the bills and work to care for their children. They have no time to spend with each other.

The PHQ revealed that his parents had divorced when he was fourteen and that his father had been an alcoholic. Amy did not want him to consume alcohol, afraid that he would also become an addict. So he had not had a single drink since their daughter was born eight years earlier.

Jack's MCHQ confirmed what Amy had written: They had not read a book, attended a seminar, or seen a counselor for marital problems.

When I scored Jack's LBI (see appendix A), the results confirmed my suspicion. His total score was 46, which when divided by 20 leaves a quotient of 2.3. That score suggested that he was in love with Amy, since it was above 1.8. His answer to question 21, "I am in love with Amy," was 3 (definitely yes), which settled the issue.

On the three forms of the *Memorandum of Agreement* that I had already started to complete with Amy's assessment, I added Jack's information. On page 2 that lists emotional needs the wife agrees to meet, I entered Sexual Fulfillment, Physical Attractiveness, Recreational Companionship, Family Commitment, and Admiration on lines 1–5. I put an asterisk before "Sexual Fulfillment," indicating that it was an unmet emotional need for Jack.

On page 3 that lists Love Busters that the wife agrees to avoid, I entered Selfish Demands, Angry Outbursts, Independent Behavior, Annoying Habits, Dishonesty, and Disrespectful Judgments on lines 1–6. I added no asterisks because Jack had no complaints regarding any of the six categories.

I told Jack that I would help Amy meet his need for sexual fulfillment, but it would require his cooperation. Without hesitation, he agreed to do whatever it took for her to become a willing sex partner.

Before I invited Amy to join us, I told Jack what I would require of him. I explained that I wanted him to learn to avoid any and all disrespectful judgments toward her and to learn to be more affectionate. He agreed to do his best

I asked Jack to wait in my office while I brought Amy to join us.

Setting Goals

After Amy was seated, I began by describing the presenting complaint—the reason Amy had made the appointment. The way Amy

131

had stated it was: "I hate having sex with Jack but I feel guilty when I turn him down." However, I didn't frame her problem in the way she presented it. Instead, I explained to both of them that Amy had wanted help to improve their sexual relationship. They both agreed that it would be their primary goal while counseling with me.

Then I described my basic assumption, the Love Bank, to both of them. I explained that everything they do affects each other, creating Love Bank account balances. If they affect each other positively, they build positive balances that, if large enough, break through the romantic love threshold. But if they affect each other negatively, they make Love Bank withdrawals that can cause them to dislike or even hate each other. In helping them achieve their goal of improved sex, I would encourage them to make large Love Bank deposits and avoid making withdrawals.

I reviewed the forms that they had both completed, beginning with the ENQ. I briefly described the questionnaire as a way to determine how they could make the largest Love Bank deposits.

Beginning with Amy, I described what Jack's ENQ had revealed. She could make the most Love Bank deposits by meeting his emotional needs for sexual fulfillment, physical attraction, and recreational companionship. Since she was already meeting his need for physical attractiveness, we would try to improve sexual fulfillment that we had already discussed. I reserved the right to address recreational companionship later.

The results of Amy's ENQ identified unequivocally that affection was her most important emotional need, and it was not being met to her satisfaction. Briefly I defined the need for Jack and explained that when he met it for Amy, he would make very large deposits into his account in her Love Bank.

I pointed out to them that Jack's number 1 emotional need, sexual fulfillment, wasn't listed among Amy's top five needs. And Amy's number 1 emotional need, affection, was not among Jack's top five. I explained that the most important emotional needs of men and women are usually very different, and that one of the great challenges of marriage is to meet an important emotional need of your spouse that isn't as important to you.

The next form I reviewed was the LBQ that revealed how Love Bank withdrawals were being made. I explained to them that my analysis led me to conclude that only Jack was making significant withdrawals. They were occurring when he made disrespectful judgments. Briefly I described disrespectful judgments and said that I would help him overcome them.

I mentioned that the MPA form that they'd both completed confirmed the conclusions reached by the ENQ and LBQ forms.

To formalize the goals that were set, I showed them the three copies of the *Memorandum of Agreement* that I had completed during the assessment. I read the entire agreement to them, which included each of their goals. Jack was to meet Amy's emotional need for affection and eliminate disrespectful judgments. Amy was to meet Jack's emotional need for sexual fulfillment.

After reading the MOA to them, I asked them both to sign my three copies, and I gave each of them a copy to take home with them. I kept the third copy for my records.

I use the PHQ to obtain a quick background check for myself on every client I counsel. But I've found that much of the information they provide is often unknown to each other and that there's great value in sharing this information and discussing it together. So, with their permission, I made a copy of their PHQs so they could take them home to read.

I also made a copy of their ENQ and LBQ for them to take with them. I encouraged them to discuss their answers with each other.

But I did not give them the results of the LBI. I explained that these results would be for my use only in determining if they were making progress. I did not want them to discuss their answers with each other and I would not reveal their scores.

The Treatment Plan

We were now ready to discuss the most important part of the assessment—the treatment plan. What should Amy and Jack do to reach their goals?

1. The Canvas—Fifteen Hours of Undivided Attention Each Week

The first, and most important, part of Amy and Jack's treatment plan was to schedule enough time to complete assignments and practice new skills. I repeated what I had told them during the intake, that I require a minimum of fifteen hours a week from the couples I counsel, so they scheduled this time together while in my office.

If a couple will not schedule fifteen hours a week to improve their marriage, I don't go any further with them in therapy. I ask them to return when they find the time to do the work I'll be assigning them. As you will discover, my assignments require at least that much time to complete, and couples who are unwilling to commit those hours rarely fulfill their marital goals.

I explained to Amy and Jack that, at first, most of their scheduled fifteen hours were to be used to complete their assignments. But as they reached their goals, I expected them to continue to schedule the time for undivided attention for the rest of their lives. I told them that the time they scheduled to be together was like a blank canvas. They would eventually be painting a beautiful scene as they learned to meet each other's emotional needs during that time. But without the canvas, the scene couldn't be created.

2. The Assignments

When Amy and Jack had scheduled fifteen hours to complete their first week's assignments, I gave them copies of my books *His Needs, Her Needs; Love Busters;* and *Five Steps to Romantic Love.* Their first reading assignment was chapters 16 (Building Romantic Love with Care) and 17 (Building Romantic Love with Time) in *Love Busters.* They were to read these chapters together.

I also made them a copy of the *Time for Undivided Attention Worksheet* found on page 184 of *Five Steps to Romantic Love.* In the "Planned Time Together" column, I wrote the dates and time of the fifteen hours they had just scheduled. I didn't write directly on the form in the workbook because it had to be used to make a clean copy every week to report their time together. I asked them to complete the remaining parts of the form and return it at the next session.

Generally, I focus a couple's attention on eliminating Love Busters before creating skill in meeting emotional needs. So for this week, their second assignment was to read chapter 4 (Disrespectful Judgments) in *Love Busters.* After reading that chapter, they were to read page 48 (Overcoming Disrespectful Judgments) in *Five Steps to Romantic Love.* Then Amy and Jack were to make two copies of the form *Disrespectful Judgments Inventory* on pages 49–50. Each would complete a copy. That form gave Amy an opportunity to explain to Jack what she considered disrespectful and how it affected her. I also asked them to review Amy's answers on the "Disrespectful Judgments" page of the *Love Busters Questionnaire* that had been completed for the assessment.

The next form *Strategy to Replace Disrespectful Judgments with Respectful Persuasion* on pages 51–52 of *Five Steps to Romantic Love* was to be completed by both Jack and Amy. Then they were to practice the strategy they had agreed to follow by completing the form *Guidelines to Respectful Persuasion Inventory* on page 53. They were to make copies of this form since they would be using it several times. Finally, they were to both cite examples of disrespectful judgments and respectful persuasion by completing the worksheets on pages 54 and 55. These forms were also to be copied so they could be used repeatedly.

All of these assignments were given to Jack and Amy in writing and were also recorded in my notes.

I explained that in the weeks to come we would focus attention on meeting the emotional needs of affection and sexual fulfillment. Amy's presenting complaint would be addressed at that time.

Before they left the waiting room, my secretary gave them an appointment card for the following week and she told them they would receive a reminder call two days before their next appointment. At that time she would ask them if they had completed their assignments. (I postpone a session if the assignments are not completed.) Also my secretary asked them to arrive fifteen minutes before their appointment so we would be able to begin on time. As a rule, if a couple comes late, I reschedule them unless my next hour is not filled.

To fit the third part of the assessment—conclusions and treatment plan—into one hour requires practice. At first, you may need two hours to complete it correctly.

The entire marital assessment should take no longer than three hours, but on some occasions, when a couple presents many difficult and complicated problems to solve, I have used as many as five hours to complete it. In those cases a second assessment session is scheduled.

You should tell a couple in advance, after you've completed their assessment, how many sessions you expect will be needed for their full recovery. The more Love Busters there are to overcome and the more emotional needs there are to learn to meet, the more sessions will be required. After using the method I propose in this book for a while, you will become increasingly accurate in your estimate.

12

Treatment

The first two sessions of marital counseling identified the problems that Jack and Amy faced. At the conclusion of the second session, they were given assignments based on a plan to overcome one of their problems, Jack's disrespectful judgments. Their treatment had begun.

Normally I divide each of the treatment sessions into four parts: thirty minutes to talk to each spouse separately, fifteen minutes together to conclude the session, and fifteen minutes to complete my notes. I take twenty minutes with the first spouse and only ten with the second because I review all of the worksheets during my interview with the first spouse. If I don't watch my time carefully during the fifteen minutes to conclude the session, the fifteen minutes reserved for my notes gets squeezed out. The time goes by very quickly, so a counselor must be highly organized to fit everything into one hour.

Since the treatment phase of the therapy is largely educational, most of the lesson material must be communicated to a couple between sessions. I do not have nearly enough time during the session to communicate what the couple needs to learn to solve their problem. So the session is designed to guide them to a lesson that will achieve that objective and then hold them accountable to complete the lesson.

Session 3: Treatment for Disrespectful Judgments

For the third session I asked to speak with Amy first because she was the one who complained about Jack's disrespectful judgments. She brought the forms with her that they had completed, and after she was seated, I began to review them.

Amy and Jack's Progress

The first form I read was the *Time for Undivided Attention Worksheet*. They had scheduled fifteen hours to complete their assignments but actually spent seventeen hours together. They used twelve hours to complete the assignments and took another five hours practicing the undivided attention they'd read about in chapter 16 of *Love Busters*. They spent part of the time talking and part of the time making love.

Amy was very encouraged. Her husband had followed through on his part of the assignments I'd given them, and that made significant Love Bank deposits into his account. She told me that by reading chapters 16 and 17 in *Love Busters*, they could both see how they had been neglecting each other's emotional needs. So they had both made a commitment to avoid letting anything rob them of their time together in the future.

She also felt that the disrespectful judgments assignments were very helpful. By completing the *Disrespectful Judgments Inventory* (part B of each question), she was given an opportunity to explain what Jack was doing that she regarded as disrespectful. The quiz on page 86 in *Love Busters* hit the nail on the head for her. She answered yes to all six questions. She entered them and other forms of disrespect on the DJI.

Instead of responding with defensiveness, Jack had taken her complaints to heart and promised that he would learn to avoid each form of disrespect that she had identified. In completing the *Strategy to Replace Disrespectful Judgments with Respectful Persuasion*, Jack was able to understand when and why he was disrespectful, and they worked together on how to practice the alternative, respectful persuasion.

I asked Amy how she had felt about making love that week, and she told me that it was her way of rewarding Jack for his effort. She didn't enjoy it but she felt he deserved it.

Jack's Session

When it was Jack's turn, I began by congratulating him on a job well done. He had taken Amy's complaints seriously and given her confidence that the drain on his Love Bank account would be stopped. But I didn't tell him that she was probably not in love with him yet.

It was relatively easy for Jack to learn to avoid disrespectful judgments because he was in love with Amy. He didn't realize that they were draining his account in her Love Bank. Had Amy been disrespectful in response to his disrespect, he would probably have lost his love for her, and as a result, the issue would have been more difficult for him to address.

Amy's answers to the questionnaires they had completed gave him an understanding of what he was doing that hurt her and what he had to do to remedy the problem. Had he not been in love, I would have had to handle his defensiveness and all of the negative fallout that it creates.

Since they both seemed well on their way to overcoming Jack's disrespectful judgments, they were ready to address emotional needs. I told Jack to remain in my office and asked Amy to join us.

New Assignments

I praised them both for the effort they had devoted to the assignments, and asked them to complete another copy of the *Time for Undivided Attention Worksheet* for their next appointment. I suggested that they try to schedule their fifteen hours for the same days and times of the day every week, since it would be easier to remember.

Their first assignment for the following week was for Jack to continue in his effort to avoid disrespectful judgments. Amy was to complete a new *Disrespectful Judgments Worksheet* and *Respectful Persuasion Worksheet* to hold him accountable. The education phase of solving this problem had essentially ended, and Jack had now entered the practice phase. He was changing his habit of being disrespectful to a habit of being respectful.

Then I introduced a new assignment—meeting Amy's emotional need for affection.

Jack was disappointed. He wanted me to focus on his need for sexual fulfillment. But first, I had to create the environment that would make it easier for Amy to make love to Jack. And I explained this to both of them. They could make love that week if Amy was willing, but I wanted Jack to create the environment of affection and to make more Love Bank deposits before I addressed Amy's reluctance to make love.

I asked them both to read the preface, introduction, and chapters 1, 2, and 3 (Affection) in *His Needs, Her Needs*. Then they were to answer "Questions for Him," "Questions for Her," and "To Consider Together" at the end of chapter 3.

After completing the assignment, they were to read Learning to Meet the Need of Affection on pages 113–14 in *Five Steps to Romantic Love*. Following that reading, Amy was to complete the *Affection Inventory* on pages 115–16 where she would describe affectionate habits she would like Jack to create and affectionate habits she wanted him to avoid. Then Jack, with Amy's assistance, was to complete the form *Strategy to Meet the Need of Affection* on pages 117–18. Finally, Amy was to make a copy of the *Affection Worksheet* on page 119 and use it to record instances during the week of Jack's showing affection and her emotional reaction. She needed to use a copy of the form rather than the original form because she would need additional copies to help her hold Jack accountable each week. All of these assignments were written on a sheet of paper that Jack and Amy took home with them, and also recorded in my notes.

When I led them back to the waiting room, my secretary gave them an appointment card for our next session, which was the following week, and told them she would call two days before to remind them of their appointment and ask if they had given each other a minimum of fifteen hours of undivided attention and if their assignments had been completed. If the fifteen hours had not been given and/or assignments were not completed, a new appointment would be scheduled to give them time to correct the problem.

Session 4: Treatment for Affection

Jack and Amy were now following two treatment plans: one to overcome Jack's disrespectful judgments and another to overcome his failure to meet Amy's need for affection.

It's risky to make only one spouse the focus of change, but in this case, I didn't have much choice. Jack was in love with Amy, but she wasn't in love with him. To remedy that imbalance, Jack had to make more Love Bank deposits and avoid making so many withdrawals. Amy didn't have to do anything but cooperate with his effort to change.

Jack's Progress

I asked Jack to come into my office first, and he handed me the forms he and Amy had completed during the week. The *Time for Undivided Attention Worksheet* indicated they had scheduled fifteen hours either to work together on their assignments or give each other undivided attention; they had followed the schedule and had made love twice during the week.

My review of the *Disrespectful Judgments Worksheet* and *Respectful Persuasion Worksheet* that Amy had completed that week reflected the fact that it was easier for Jack to avoid being disrespectful than it was for him to discuss an issue with Amy respectfully. His solution to the issue of disrespect was simply to avoid disagreeing with her. There was only one entry on the *Disrespectful Judgments Worksheet*—Jack had rolled his eyes when Amy thought he was driving too fast. But there were no entries on the *Respectful Persuasion Worksheet*.

They had not discussed any conflicts that week. I asked Jack to try to think, after he returned to the waiting room, of any topics of conflict that existed between him and Amy. I gave him a few categories: conflicts concerning friends and relatives, time management, financial planning, and child discipline.

The *Affection Inventory* that Amy completed gave Jack a clear vision of what affection meant to her. She wanted him to hug her, hold her hand, and tell her he loved her more often. When they sat together at home watching television together, she wanted him to run his fingers through her hair and rub her feet occasionally. She wanted gifts to be more sentimental—jewelry occasionally. What she didn't want was groping and grabbing when they were together. She felt as if she had to guard her body whenever he was close to her.

Jack had completed the *Strategy to Meet the Need of Affection* form, where he acknowledged the way Amy wanted him to show affection and suggested a plan that would help him learn to be more affectionate. He took the advice from chapter 3 of *His Needs, Her Needs* and made a list of affectionate behaviors he would practice every day.

Amy had agreed to the plan and documented instances of his affection and her reaction to them on the *Affection Worksheet*. They had just started the plan three days earlier, but Amy felt that it was already working well.

My approach to solving almost every marital problem begins by creating new behavior, and that can seem very contrived at first. Jack had never been a very affectionate husband, and his initial efforts at holding Amy's hand, hugging her without groping, telling her he loved her, running his fingers through her hair, and rubbing her feet seemed very awkward. But Amy's need for affection made her enjoy even his awkward efforts. And the longer he practiced the affectionate habits, the smoother he would become.

I took Jack back to the waiting room and reminded him to think of examples of conflicts. Then I led Amy back to my office.

Amy's Satisfaction

Amy was beaming. She told me that she had not felt this close to Jack in years but was afraid that it wouldn't last. Would he continue to be respectful and affectionate or would he eventually revert back to the unromantic husband he'd always been?

The first time Amy had made love to Jack that week, she did it to reward him for the changes he was making, just as she had the week earlier. But she didn't hate doing it this time. Then when she made love to him a second time that week, she actually enjoyed it. She felt emotionally connected and was able to express her feelings for him sexually.

I asked Amy how she felt taking up the topic of sexual fulfillment next. She had already looked ahead in the workbook and thought the forms she would be completing would be very helpful to both of them.

When Jack joined us, I reviewed what they had achieved so far. Disrespectful judgments had been reduced to almost zero, and affection was off to a very good start. But respectful persuasion was something that Jack felt very uneasy trying to attempt. He was afraid that if he were to disagree with Amy, the magic that they had now created would disappear.

He had a point. Even when disagreements are respectful, there's a risk of making Love Bank withdrawals. And yet no married couple can get far in life without skill in resolving conflicts. Somehow Jack had to be able to express disagreement and do it in a respectful way.

New Assignments

I told Amy that I'd asked Jack to think of a few unresolved issues while he was in the waiting room. He told us that he had identified three—when to visit his parents, when and how to punish their children, and when to buy new bedroom furniture. If he were to agree to the way Amy wanted to handle each of these issues, he'd be making Love Bank deposits into his account, but they wouldn't be the way he would want the issues addressed. In other words, her gain would be at his loss. I told them that I wanted them to learn how to resolve conflicts so that deposits would be made into both of their accounts.

We didn't have time to deal with the three issues that week, but by introducing them with the goal of mutual agreement, they would be thinking about them.

This week's assignment was to add one more skill that would help build their Love Bank accounts: Sexual Fulfillment.

First, they were to read chapter 4 (Sexual Fulfillment) in *His Needs, Her Needs*. After reading the chapter, they were to answer

"Questions for Him," "Questions for Her," and "To Consider Together."

Then they were to read Learning to Meet the Need of Sexual Fulfillment on pages 120–21 in *Five Steps to Romantic Love*. Following that reading, Amy was to complete the *Sexual Experience Inventory* on pages 122–26 where she would describe conditions that trigger each of the five stages of the sexual experience for her. Then together they were to complete the form *Strategy to Discover the Five Stages of Sexual Experience* on page 127. Finally, Amy was to make five copies of the *Sexual Experience Worksheet* on page 128, one for each of the five stages.

There are more forms in the sexual fulfillment section of the workbook, but I don't use them unless a couple is still sexually unfulfilled after completing this first assignment.

In addition to this week's assignment, I reminded them that the *Time for Undivided Attention Worksheet,* the *Disrespectful Judgments Worksheet,* the *Respectful Persuasion Worksheet*, and the *Affection Worksheet* were also to be completed. They began to wonder if fifteen hours would be enough time to complete them all. I suggested that they might prefer to schedule their next appointment for two weeks away instead of one. After Amy had seen all of the worksheets she would need to complete, and imagining the effort it would take on her part to understand her own reactions in each of the five stages of the sexual response, she agreed. The assignments I gave them were listed on a sheet of paper for Jack and Amy to take with them, and were also recorded in my notes.

My secretary reminded them again that she would call them two days before their next appointment to ask if they had given fifteen hours of undivided attention to each other each week and if their assignments had been completed. I suggested that she also call them in a week to ask if they were on target with their assignments and with spending fifteen hours together.

Session 5: Treatment for Sexual Fulfillment

A month had passed since I'd asked Amy and Jack to complete the *Love Bank Inventory*, so when they arrived for their appointment fifteen minutes early, my secretary gave each of them a copy of the form to complete. She asked them to go to separate parts of the waiting room so they would not see each other's answers.

Amy and Jack's Progress

I asked Amy to follow me to my office, and when she was seated, I scored her LBI. Her first Love Bank quotient after the assessment had been 0.3, a barely positive score, and well below the romantic love threshold of 1.8. This time, however, her quotient was 2.1, which was above the threshold. The rating she gave to the item, "I am in love with Jack," was 3 (definitely yes).

By Jack's eliminating disrespectful judgments that had been draining his account in her Love Bank, and making deposits by meeting her need for affection, she was now in love with him.

As I reviewed the forms they had completed during the past two weeks, I saw they had spent at least fifteen hours together each week either completing the assignments or giving each other undivided attention.

Disrespectful judgments had been essentially eliminated, and they had spent some time practicing respectful persuasion. The topic they chose to discuss was buying bedroom furniture. Amy wanted new furniture because they had no headboard, and their dresser, mirror, and nightstands didn't match. She also mentioned to Jack that new furniture would put her in a better mood for sex. Before discussing the issue, Jack believed they couldn't afford it, but her second argument was so convincing that he enthusiastically agreed to order a new bedroom set that week.

The *Affection Worksheet* indicated that Jack was following their plan to meet Amy's need for affection, and her response to his efforts had been very positive. He was starting to be more spontaneous and natural in the way he expressed his affection, and that brought out an even more positive response in her.

When I reviewed the sexual fulfillment forms Amy had completed, she was all smiles. "We made love six times since we saw you last," she said. "I'm not sure we'll need to come for counseling much longer because I don't feel the same way I felt about sex a few weeks ago."

The five stages of the sexual response are each analyzed in the *Sexual Experience Inventory*. Amy's answers to the questions regarding the first stage, sexual willingness, said it all for her. For several years, she had been unwilling to make love to Jack because she didn't feel emotionally bonded to him. But occasionally she would reluctantly agree because she felt that he needed it. Her reluctance to make love prevented her from fully experiencing the remaining stages—arousal, plateau, climax, and recovery. She would go through the motions without actually having an enjoyable sexual experience.

Granted, Jack had a few problems with his sexual technique that Amy explained in the remainder of the inventory. But her general unwillingness, caused by a lack of emotional connection, would have made almost any technique fail. Her unwillingness did not mean that she refused to have sex with him. It meant that she didn't emotionally participate in the other stages of the sexual experience.

Now that she felt bonded to Jack, because he avoided disrespectful judgments and had become affectionate, she was willing to have sex with him. Once she became a willing partner, she was then able to explain to Jack what he could do to make it easier for her to enjoy the other four stages of the sexual experience.

Occasionally I'll come across a woman who is willing to make love but simply doesn't know how to experience arousal, plateau, and climax due to a lack of experience. In those cases, I encourage her to learn how to enjoy each stage and then train her husband in lovemaking positions and techniques that maximize her pleasure.

But in Amy's case, once she had cracked the willingness stage, the rest was easy for her.

As I mentioned earlier, there are two conditions that should be met if a wife is to be enthusiastically willing to meet her husband's need for sexual fulfillment. First, she must feel emotionally connected to him, and second, she must enjoy the experience. The first condition had now been met, because being in love and feeling emotionally connected are similar concepts in marriage. And once the first condition was met, Amy already knew how to enjoy the experience. She was now willing to make love to Jack just about whenever he wanted.

Jack's Response

I escorted Amy to the waiting room and led Jack to my office. After scoring his LBI, I discovered that the effort he'd made to be more affectionate and overcome disrespectful judgments had taken a small toll on Amy's account. His score four weeks earlier had been 2.3, well above the romantic love threshold of 1.8. But now it had dropped to 2.0, still above the threshold, but not as high.

The approach I take, to build up the lower Love Bank balance first, is often at the expense of the higher Love Bank balance. When someone changes his or her habits, it takes effort, and effort is often somewhat unpleasant. Jack wanted Amy to be happy with him and to feel better about making love, but avoiding disrespectful judgments and learning how to be affectionate were hard work for him.

As is usually the case, the gains to Jack's account were far greater than the losses to Amy's account. His account went from 0.3 to 2.1, an increase of 1.8, while Amy's loss was only 0.3. They were now both in love, but Jack's Love Bank balance was slightly lower than Amy's.

You might have thought that Amy's new willingness to make love to Jack would have more than balanced out the losses to her account in his Love Bank. But our discussion explained why that didn't happen.

"How do you feel about the way the week went?" I asked Jack.

"It went okay, but I feel like Amy is analyzing me under a microscope," he responded. "It's keeping me on my toes, though. First, it was about disrespectful judgments and then she evaluated my affection. Now, she's being critical of the way we have sex."

This is the reason I see spouses separately. If Amy had heard how Jack had reacted to her advice regarding the best ways to make love to her, she would have been so offended that she might have discontinued the lessons. But I was able to explain to Jack that I wanted them to meet each other's emotional needs, and Amy knew more about what worked for her sexually than anyone.

We also had a brief discussion about what he could and could not expect from Amy. He wanted oral sex and even anal sex once in a while. But Amy found both of those practices to be disgusting. I explained that they were to meet each other's emotional needs in a mutually enjoyable way. Any form of sex that was unpleasant for either of them had to be avoided, regardless of how much enjoyment the other person would experience.

After congratulating Jack on another job well done, I went to the waiting room to ask Amy to join us.

Assignments

Even though Amy had expressed a desire to end counseling now that she no longer hated having sex with Jack, I encouraged them to stick with the program. I mentioned that what goes up fast can also come down fast. The gains they had made could be reversed if they stopped, or even slowed down, in their pursuit of a great marriage. They agreed, so I gave them their new assignments.

The conflict over bedroom furniture had been resolved with enthusiastic agreement, so I suggested that this time they focus attention on the conflict over when to visit Jack's parents.

I reminded them that the *Time for Undivided Attention Worksheet*, the *Disrespectful Judgments Worksheet*, the *Respectful Persuasion Worksheet*, and the *Affection Worksheet* were also to be completed. I gave them no worksheet to record their reactions to their lovemaking, but I wanted them to record the number of times they made love. I encouraged them to make love as often as either of them took the initiative, but it had to be done in a way that was mutually enjoyable.

I scheduled their next appointment in three weeks. For the remaining sessions, they would consolidate their gains. They would practice until their new behavior became almost effortless.

As they were about to leave the waiting room, my secretary gave them an appointment card and told them she would call once a week to check up on them. And then two days before their next appointment, she would call to ask if their worksheets were being completed and if they were spending fifteen hours each week giving each other undivided attention.

13

Practice and Discharge

The first two sessions I had with Amy and Jack were devoted to assessing their problems and creating goals. Each of the next three sessions implemented a treatment plan to achieve one of their three goals: Jack overcoming disrespectful judgments, Jack learning how to meet Amy's need for affection, and Amy learning to meet his need for sexual fulfillment. At the conclusion of the fifth session, Jack was no longer being disrespectful and he was meeting Amy's need for affection. Amy was meeting his need for sexual fulfillment. They were in love with each other.

By that time, Amy and Jack both felt their therapy was a success and that they should be discharged. Many therapists would have agreed with them. But while it seemed that their problem was solved, they were really only halfway finished. What remained was to turn their changed behavior into habits.

They were making an effort to follow the plan and they were reaping the rewards of changed behavior, but my goal for them was to make the changes permanent. I wanted his effort to avoid disrespect, his effort to show her affection, and her effort to meet his need for sexual fulfillment to become almost effortless for both of them. That would require practice and lots of it.

So for the next four sessions, I would hold Amy and Jack accountable to practice the new behavior they'd learned. If they maintained their practice, each session would be spaced out farther from the last. The exception would be setbacks. In such cases, I might not increase the time between sessions and even shorten the time until they were on track again. When we would finally reach the tenth session, about two years after intake, their discharge would be appropriate—their new behavior would have become solid habits.

Session 6: Practicing Respectful Persuasion, Affection, and Sexual Fulfillment

I met Jack and Amy in the waiting room and asked them who would like to talk with me first. Jack volunteered and he brought their worksheets with him. I left a copy of the *Love Bank Inventory* for Amy to complete while she was waiting.

Jack's Progress

Jack sat down and I began reading their worksheets. There was a separate worksheet for each week since I had last seen them.

The *Time for Undivided Attention Worksheets* indicated that they had scheduled, and actually spent, at least fifteen hours each week meeting each other's emotional needs for affection, sexual fulfillment, intimate conversation, and recreational companionship. They had made love eleven times during the past three weeks.

The *Disrespectful Judgments Worksheets* indicated that Jack had been making an effort to avoid saying or doing anything that Amy regarded as disrespectful. One week there had been no instances of disrespectful judgments, and during the other two weeks, there had been only one each week. In those two cases, Jack had taken note of what Amy had interpreted as being disrespectful and he had apologized. Both times he had been teasing her, but she did not think it was funny.

Humor is often disrespectful, and when spouses make fun of each other, even with no harm intended, it's rarely considered harmless. I explained to Jack that in an intimate relationship, spouses are particularly vulnerable to each other and are usually very sensitive. When you're in love, it's easy to be a bull in a china closet—you should be careful how you navigate. Finding humor in something your spouse does can be like knocking over a crystal vase.

I reviewed the *Respectful Persuasion Worksheets* that are companions to the *Disrespectful Judgments Worksheets*. Previously they had been left blank, but this time they were completed because a conflict had been discussed.

1. Resolving Conflict

I had asked Jack and Amy to try to resolve a conflict—when to visit his parents. The purpose of the exercise was to negotiate a resolution with respect. Opinions of both spouses were to be discussed and fully understood. Then proposals were to be presented that would take those opinions into account. They were allowed to try to change each other's opinions, but it had to be done without giving the impression that they were being disrespectful.

Jack had wanted to visit his parents more often and for longer periods of time than Amy had felt comfortable. They lived three hours away, and a visit would ordinarily take at least an entire day. But the real problem was that invariably his three brothers and their wives, who lived near his parents, would come over after they arrived. And they brought with them beer, crude jokes, and nonstop disrespect—for everyone and everything. Amy found the scene intolerable.

Jack's tendency to be disrespectful was not a reflection of his lack of respect for Amy—he was in love and considered himself to be very fortunate to be married to her. Instead, it was something he'd learned growing up in his family. Everyone made fun of everyone else. And their jokes were often sexist and racist. Even when jokes were not directed at her, Amy felt they were very inappropriate.

Jack wasn't comfortable telling his brothers not to visit when he came to see his parents and he certainly could not ask them to be more sensitive when Amy was around. He was afraid that if he raised that issue, they would think it particularly humorous and would talk about it in her presence. And Amy refused to put up with his family if they were to talk the way they did.

In the three weeks since I'd seen them, they had not resolved this issue. But Jack had not been disrespectful in discussing it with Amy, either. She was starting to persuade him that his family's jibes were not very funny if they were at the expense of others, particularly those who were present.

2. Showing Affection

Jack had done a magnificent job according to the *Affection Worksheet*. The list of affectionate behaviors that Amy had given him was followed every day, and he was starting to be creative. He called her more often from work to see how she was doing. That helped keep her in his thoughts throughout the day. Every call was a way of saying, "I'm here for you when you need me."

Because Jack was thinking about Amy more often, he did more for her. He picked things up for her that she needed on his way home from work, and while he was at it, he would include a card or flowers that expressed his care. When he kissed her, it would not be a peck on the cheek. It would be a passionate expression of his love. He held her hand when they stood next to each other and he hugged her with conviction.

Sex was no longer a problem. When they were in bed together, sex was a natural extension of the affection they had expressed to each other throughout the day. It had become lovemaking.

Amy's Progress

I led Jack to the waiting room and gave him a copy of *Love Bank Inventory* to complete while he was waiting. Amy followed me to my office and gave me the copy she had finished. I scored it immediately and found Jack's Love Bank quotient to have risen to 2.5, 0.4 points higher than the score had been three weeks earlier. Jack's account in her Love Bank was getting close to the ceiling of 3.0. I didn't reveal the score to her, but she already knew that her feelings toward him were still improving.

We discussed Jack's family and how disrespectful they were. Amy was very impressed with his success in breaking away from family tradition but was still unwilling to visit his family or even agree to let him visit by himself. She felt they were all a very bad influence on him and that a visit might trigger his old habits.

Assignments

I asked Amy to wait in my office while I invited Jack to join us. When he arrived I scored the LBI that he had completed while he was in the waiting room. Amy's account in his Love Bank had improved. Her Love Bank quotient rose to 2.7 from 2.0. His effort to avoid disrespectful judgments and to create an environment of affection required much less effort, hence fewer withdrawals from Amy's account. His practice was turning respect and affection into habits. And Amy's passionate and frequent lovemaking was making a huge deposit into her account. He asked about his score, but I reminded him that it was the one piece of information that I could not reveal to them. I added that if he wanted Amy to know how much he loved her, he would just have to tell her.

I congratulated them both for a job well done and told them that I'd be spacing their appointments out farther and farther until I discharged them. The next appointment would be in six weeks.

They were to continue to complete the *Time for Undivided Attention Worksheet*, the *Disrespectful Judgments Worksheet*, the *Respectful Persuasion Worksheet*, and the *Affection Worksheet*. Before I let them go, I suggested that they try to resolve the third conflict that Jack had mentioned, when and how to discipline their children.

Amy and Jack had not yet resolved their second conflict, visiting Jack's parents, but I felt that they were going about it correctly. They were following the Policy of Joint Agreement (never do anything without an enthusiastic agreement between you and your spouse), which meant that they wouldn't visit Jack's parents until they had an agreement.

Not all conflicts must be resolved for a couple to be in love, as was evidenced by the fact that they were in love, yet had not resolved two of the three conflicts Jack had named. Jack was willing to forgo seeing his parents for a while if it meant having a better relationship with Amy. He was also willing to let her call the shots regarding child discipline for the same reason. But I wanted them to learn how to come to an enthusiastic agreement and not resort to capitulation. So for the next six weeks, they would spend some of their time together each week discussing their child-rearing methods.

Before they left my office, I warned them that disrespectful judgments can be very difficult to eliminate, particularly when conflicts are emotionally charged. If they found themselves being disrespectful when discussing child-rearing methods, they should drop the issue until they saw me for their next appointment.

My secretary gave them an appointment card and said she would give them a reminder call two days before their next appointment. As in the past, she would ask if they had given each other a minimum of fifteen hours a week of undivided attention and completed their worksheets.

Session 7: Practicing Respectful Persuasion, Affection, and Sexual Fulfillment

When Amy and Jack came for their seventh session, Amy volunteered to meet with me first. I gave Jack a copy of the LBI to complete while he was waiting for his turn. Amy brought all of the worksheets they had completed over the past six weeks into my office.

Spontaneous Recovery

Spontaneous recovery is a term psychologists use to describe a phenomenon frequently seen during the development of a new habit. Suddenly and without any apparent warning, the old habit reappears. As I reviewed the *Disrespectful Judgments Worksheets*, it became apparent that the progress Jack had made overcoming disrespect had eroded. His habit of making disrespectful judgments had recovered spontaneously, and the worksheets proved it.

Amy told me that the breakdown occurred when they were discussing child-rearing methods. Until that point Amy had usually made the decisions when it came to discipline.

Spontaneous Recovery: When an old habit reappears suddenly and without any apparent warning.

When either of their children, Jessica (8) or Ryan (6), would occasionally disobey her, she would spank the offender. But she always followed the spanking with hugs and kisses so that the children knew she loved them. Jack didn't think they deserved spankings but didn't interfere.

So when the issue finally came up as an exercise in respectful persuasion, Amy expected Jack to express his opinion that children should not be spanked but she expected him to do it in a respectful way. That didn't happen.

The conversation started out respectfully, with each of them explaining their opinion regarding discipline. Amy said she felt that if their children were not spanked, they would become increasingly disobedient, and eventually she would not be able to control them. Jack disagreed, expressing his opinion that children who were spanked were learning to solve problems with violence. He preferred a nonviolent approach to discipline, such as sending children to their rooms for a time-out.

At the beginning, it seemed as if their conflicting opinions could be discussed respectfully. But Jack made the first mistake when he said that Amy was taking the "easy way out" by spanking and that using nonviolent methods takes more wisdom and energy. This was a disrespectful thing to say, and Amy wrote it down on her DJW. She suggested that they discuss the issue at a later time, after she had a chance to cool off.

But Jack didn't want to end the discussion. He felt Amy should listen to what he had to say. After telling her that if she didn't agree with his position on discipline, their children's lives might be ruined, he started lecturing her on the value of nonviolence. When Amy had finally run out of space on the DJW, she left the room.

Fortunately, the negotiation that turned into an argument didn't ruin the progress they had made. A day later Jack apologized for being disrespectful and suggested they wait for their next appointment before bringing up the issue of child discipline again.

The *Affection Worksheets* indicated that after Jack's apology, they had returned to expressing their affection to each other. And their lovemaking continued to be frequent and passionate.

I asked Amy how she was feeling about her relationship with Jack, and she expressed great optimism. She was very impressed with how

Jack had apologized for his disrespect and how quickly they were able to put the incident behind them.

Jack's LBI

I led Amy to the waiting room and gave her a copy of the LBI to complete. Jack came to my office, and I scored his LBI.

His new score was 2.6, a drop of 0.1 from his last score. While such a small decrease should not necessarily be taken as a setback, I felt that their argument may have had a small negative impact on Jack. He had handled it well by apologizing afterward, but the issue was very important to him, and I assumed that he felt he was not being heard. I did not reveal his Love Bank quotient to him nor did I discuss my assessment of the situation.

I told him what Amy had said about their child discipline argument, and he agreed with her interpretation. He knew that he'd been disrespectful when he tried to lecture her on the subject of nonviolent discipline. On the other hand, he felt that the issue should be resolved soon and he wanted it resolved in his favor.

Resolving Conflicts

After asking Jack about his general feelings concerning their progress and hearing his positive response, I went to the waiting room to ask Amy to join us. When she was seated, I quickly scored her LBI. Her score was 2.6, an increase of 0.1. The argument did not seem to have negatively affected her love for Jack, primarily because of the way he had handled the recovery. By apologizing for being disrespectful, he had turned a potentially devastating event into an encouraging outcome. Amy was impressed with the way he had acknowledged his error, which helped them both get back on track again.

I laid out their issue of child discipline as Amy had related it to me. They had conflicting opinions regarding the effect of corporal punishment on children. Amy believed it would lead to obedience, and Jack believed it would lead to violence.

We had only about ten minutes left in the session, so I had to make my points quickly. I suggested that they try again to express their opinions on the subject of discipline, but this time without any lecturing. A lecture is "telling" the other person that he or she is wrong and why the person is wrong. Instead, they should try to persuade with evidence. Why do you believe what you do? What evidence is there for your opinion?

In marriage, conflicts can exist without destroying a relationship as long as the Policy of Joint Agreement is followed (never do anything without an enthusiastic agreement between you and your spouse). If opinions don't lead to action until there is agreement, the opinions themselves rarely cause Love Bank withdrawals.

So with the POJA in mind, I suggested that during the next few weeks, neither spouse should act on his or her opinion until they agreed. In other words, they should not discipline their children without the other spouse's enthusiastic agreement. I realized that the default condition of the policy, do nothing unless you agree, meant that Jack would have his way for a while—he wanted Amy to stop spanking the children. But I told them that doing nothing prevented one spouse from making unilateral decisions and eventually it would help them come to an agreement.

Their second conflict, when and how often to spend time with Jack's parents, had not been resolved either. The default condition for that conflict, never visit Jack's parents, gave Amy what she wanted. But Amy didn't object to frequent telephone calls to his parents, and so for the time being, Jack wasn't resentful about the temporary arrangement.

I reviewed type A and type B resentment with Amy and Jack (see chapter 10). Type A is created by violating the POJA. If Amy spanked the children, Jack would feel resentful. If he visited his parents, she would feel resentful. That's type A resentment.

On the other hand, type B resentment is created when the default condition of the POJA is followed. If Amy were prevented from spanking the children, she would feel resentful, and if Jack were prevented from visiting his parents, he would feel resentful. That's type B resentment.

Type A is worse than type B resentment for a very important reason. Once an action is done, it can't be undone. Amy spanking the children was thoughtless because it ignored Jack's feelings and interests. Every time she spanked the children, he would remember it as an example of her thoughtlessness. The same would be true for her when he insisted on visiting his parents. He would be ignoring her feelings and interests, causing her to be resentful for years to come.

Type B resentment, on the other hand, is temporary, disappearing as soon as an enthusiastic agreement is reached. Amy may feel resentful while she's not allowed to spank her disobedient children, but when she and Jack find a mutually agreeable alternative, no resentment will remain. While Jack would not be able to visit his parents, he would feel resentment. But it would end as soon as the conflict was resolved.

So I encouraged Amy to avoid spanking her children until they could agree enthusiastically on a method of discipline. She was willing to follow this plan, and Jack promised he would not be disrespectful as they discussed the issue.

I reminded them that no conflict is more important than their love for each other, and that their top priority was to make massive Love Bank deposits and avoid making any withdrawals. I also reminded them that problem solving would be much easier when they paid attention to how they were affecting each other. That's what it takes to be thoughtful.

Since they had hit a small speed bump on their path to recovery, I did not expand the interval between sessions. Instead, I scheduled them for another appointment in six weeks. They were to continue to complete the *Time for Undivided Attention Worksheet*, the *Disrespectful Judgments Worksheet*, the *Respectful Persuasion Worksheet*, and the *Affection Worksheet*.

My secretary gave them an appointment card and said she would give them a reminder call two days before their next appointment. She would also ask if they had given each other a minimum of fifteen hours a week of undivided attention and completed their worksheets.

Session 8: Practicing Respectful Persuasion, Affection, and Sexual Fulfillment

Amy came to my office first for session eight and Jack remained in the waiting room, completing the LBI. Amy brought with her their copies of the *Time for Undivided Attention Worksheet*, the *Disrespectful Judgments Worksheet*, the *Respectful Persuasion Worksheet*, and the *Affection Worksheet*.

Amy and Jack's Progress

As I read through the worksheets, I could see that they had been faithful in spending a minimum of fifteen hours together each week meeting each other's needs for affection, sexual fulfillment, conversation, and recreational companionship. Jack had avoided disrespectful judgments and continued to be affectionate with Amy. When I asked her about their lovemaking, she said that from her perspective it couldn't be better.

Their *Respectful Persuasion Worksheet* showed that they had spent quite a bit of time discussing child discipline and had made considerable progress. Amy had promised not to punish their children until she had come to a mutually enthusiastic agreement with Jack, and she had stuck to her promise. That motivated her to try to come to a quick decision, and since it had to be mutually enthusiastic, she knew that she couldn't force Jack to agree with her. So they had had several respectful discussions following their children's acts of disobedience and were coming to some basic agreements regarding when and how to punish the children.

I asked Amy if there was anything she wanted to discuss in private. She said that Jack could be present to hear anything she had to say. So I led her back to the waiting room, gave her a copy of the LBI to complete, and asked Jack to join me in my office.

Jack's LBI

Jack's LBI reflected the fact that he was still very much in love with Amy. His score increased from 2.6 to 2.7, an increase of 0.1. Small increments don't necessarily reflect positive or negative change, but in this case he felt that they were doing a little better.

I asked Jack how he felt about their lovemaking and he agreed with Amy that it was terrific. He had no complaints.

All that remained to be discussed was the child discipline issue and the issue of Jack visiting his parents, so I suggested inviting Amy into the session much earlier than usual. This time we would take about one-half hour to focus attention on how to resolve conflicts.

Resolving Conflicts

During the first few sessions, I usually reserve most of the available time for talking with spouses individually because I want to know what the other spouse is doing that bothers them without creating an emotional uproar. If they were to describe their complaints in each other's presence, they might hurt each other's feelings, and they would probably leave the session feeling worse about their marriage than when they had arrived. One of my counseling goals is to encourage couples, so I don't let them criticize each other when they are together.

But during the last few sessions, I talk with them together for most of the time because by then they're not likely to be critical—they've learned how to express their complaints tactfully.

I directed Amy to my office, and she gave me her completed copy of the *Love Bank Inventory*. After quickly scoring it, I found that her Love Bank quotient was 2.6, the same as it had been six weeks earlier. Technically, I'd rather see a score of 2.6 than a score of 3.0 because it probably indicates that the spouse has been somewhat discriminating in answering the questions. I did not include a lie scale in the inventory, so a person can appear to be in love when he or she isn't. That's why quotients gained from the LBI should be validated by other evidence. In the case of Amy and Jack, the evidence was abundant. As they sat together in my office, they definitely had the look of love.

I had already read the *Respectful Persuasion Worksheets* that described their discussions regarding child discipline. They were coming to an enthusiastic agreement regarding an overall strategy to train their children. I asked them to explain it to me.

Amy volunteered. "Before counseling, each of us would discipline the children the way we saw fit. For example, when Jessica and Ryan would fight over what TV show they would watch, I'd spank them, and Jack would try to talk to them. Then we'd argue about it. But when I was unable to spank them without his agreement, they began fighting more often about almost everything. Jack saw the value of my spankings."

"But that's not the whole story, right?" interrupted Jack. "Tell Dr. Harley what you told me last week."

"I was getting to that if you'd give me a chance," said Amy with a frown.

Jack knew he had made a mistake and immediately apologized for interrupting. Jack's past tendency to be disrespectful had made a slight recovery. He had learned that interruptions were a form of disrespect and he had been trying to avoid them.

She continued, "I was beginning to think that Jack's talks combined with my spankings were probably more effective in keeping the children in line than either approach by itself. Without spanking, the talks didn't have much effect. But if I spanked them without the talks, they were learning that 'might makes right.' What would we do with them when they were teenagers? We couldn't keep spanking them then!"

After discussing the issue on several occasions, they had come to the conclusion that sometimes the only thing a child understands is a spanking. Talk doesn't always work. On the other hand, without explaining why the behavior is wrong and what they could do to handle conflicts better, a spanking alone sends the wrong message. It might lead a child to think that brute force gets results.

They were learning to respect each other's opinions. Both of them had wisdom to bring to every decision. But along with their wisdom, some foolishness is sprinkled in. The Policy of Joint Agreement was helping them discern the difference.

I made a suggestion based on my training in child psychology. Since a child's brain and accompanying cognitive skills change over time, one form of discipline may be appropriate at one stage of their development but inappropriate at another. When children are young, say eight and under, a spanking is usually effective in maintaining control. But as they mature, corporal punishment leads to oppositional behavior. The more you punish them, the more they tend to do the opposite of what you tell them to do. Amy and Jack's children were reaching an age where spankings would lose their effectiveness.

I made another suggestion. If they were both to talk to their children, their message would be far more effective than if only one of them were making the effort. Children tend to ignore the lessons of one parent when there is disagreement with the other parent.

I suggested that they read together chapter 11, Family Commit-ment, in *His Needs, Her Needs*. It stresses the importance of quality family time, when parents have an opportunity to influence their children's values. Time together as a family can have a much greater positive impact on children's behavior than spankings or lectures.

Before the end of the session, I asked them about their conflict regarding Jack visiting his parents. They both felt that progress had been made and they would test an approach to the problem. Jack and Amy would visit his parents on short notice and for only a few hours. That way the brothers would be unlikely to show up. Even if they did, it would be for a limited amount of time. If Amy felt comfortable with the visit, the problem would be solved. Otherwise, they would go back to the drawing board.

I told them that this time the only worksheets they should continue to complete were the *Time for Undivided Attention Worksheet*, the *Disrespectful Judgments Worksheet*, and the *Respectful Persuasion Worksheet*. They could skip the *Affection Worksheet* since their romantic relationship was humming right along, and affection was an integral part of their experience. As long as their Love Bank quo-tients were high, and they had fifteen hours of undivided attention that they knew were to be devoted to affection, sexual fulfillment, conversation, and recreational companionship, documentation of the details was no longer necessary.

I scheduled their next appointment for three months later. My secretary gave them an appointment card and said she would give them a reminder call two days before their next appointment. She would also be asking if they had given each other a minimum of fifteen hours a week of undivided attention and completed their worksheets.

Session 9: Preparing for Discharge

When I met Amy and Jack in the waiting room, I told them I would be spending most of the time with them together, but I wanted to see them individually for just a few minutes. Jack volunteered to be first, so I gave Amy a copy of the LBI for her to complete while she waited.

Amy and Jack's Progress

I looked through the worksheets that Jack brought with him and saw that over the three months they had maintained fifteen hours a week of undivided attention. They had continued to be affectionate and had made love very frequently. As a new recreational activity, they had chosen to go dancing one night a week, which they both enjoyed. Jack had no complaints.

I noticed that the *Disrespectful Judgments Worksheets* had an occasional entry from Amy. During the session three months earlier, Jack had interrupted her, and I had pointed out to them that it qualified as disrespect if she felt offended. From that day on, she fine-tuned her criteria for disrespectful judgments. But whenever she wrote an entry on the DJW, Jack would apologize and make a greater effort to avoid the behavior. I noticed that during the past two weeks there had been no entries.

The *Respectful Persuasion Worksheet* indicated that they had made significant progress in resolving their child discipline conflict. They had read chapter 11 (Family Commitment) in *His Needs, Her Needs* and had started to follow my advice regarding quality family time. They had scheduled more family activities with the goal of helping their children learn to cooperate with each other instead of fighting. It led to far fewer fights.

Jack mentioned the fact that they were now using the Policy of Joint Agreement whenever they had any conflict and found that they were gaining skill in coming to enthusiastic agreements about many issues.

Amy's LBI

I asked Jack to follow me back to the waiting room and gave him a copy of the LBI to complete. Then Amy came to my office, and I scored her LBI. Her earlier score of 2.6 had not changed, and she was still in love with Jack.

I asked Amy if there was anything she wanted to say before I invited Jack to join us. She said that everything was going well and she appreciated the help I had given them. So I went back to the waiting room where Jack was finishing his LBI.

Strengthening Commitment

When I returned to my office with Jack, I scored his LBI and found that the score had increased from 2.7 to 2.8. He was still in love with Amy.

I told them that this session and the next (the final session) would be designed to remind them of their commitments to each other. The two rules that I wanted them to follow for the rest of their lives were the Policy of Undivided Attention (give each other a minimum of fifteen hours a week of undivided attention to meet the needs of affection, sexual fulfillment, conversation, and recreational companionship) and the Policy of Joint Agreement (never do anything without an enthusiastic agreement between you and your spouse). Ever since they had followed these rules, their marriage had been sensational. I warned them, however, that romantic love is fragile, and when these rules are not followed, they could lose the love they had for each other.

I went on to say that a weekly schedule that is rarely broken is the friend of marriages because it helps trigger habits that have been proven to make Love Bank deposits. That's why the fifteen hours of undivided attention should be scheduled for the same time from week to week.

The habits they had learned could be temporarily forgotten when schedule changes occur during holidays and vacations. The period of time between Thanksgiving and New Year's Day is notoriously difficult for couples because they may feel too busy to take time for each other. But if a couple is too busy to do what it takes to sustain their love for each other, they're too busy to be happily married.

Interruptions in a couple's ability to meet each other's emotional needs, such as illness in the family, children out of school during the summer, a change in jobs, a move, or a new baby can be so disruptive to good marital habits that a couple may have to form them all over again. If Amy and Jack would recognize the problem before losing their love for each other, though, these habits would be much easier to restore than if they waited until their Love Banks were drained dry.

The books I'd given them, *His Needs, Her Needs; Love Busters*; and the workbook *Five Steps to Romantic Love,* could be used to help them solve any other marital problems that might arise. I encouraged them to read them from cover to cover so they would know how to approach possible future problems.

I told Amy and Jack that it would be up to them if they wanted to continue to complete the *Time for Undivided Attention Worksheet*, the *Disrespectful Judgments Worksheet*, and the *Respectful Persuasion Worksheet*. If they felt it would help them stay on track, it wouldn't take that much time for them to complete since they were in the habit of doing so.

Their final appointment was scheduled to be in one year. But I asked them to complete a *Love Bank Inventory* for my records every three months. My receptionist would send them copies that they could return by fax or mail. She would score them and give me the results during the year. If either of their scores dropped significantly, I would contact them to move up their next appointment.

An appointment card was given to them, and they were told to expect a reminder call two days before their last session.

Session 10: Discharge

During the year that passed between sessions, Amy and Jack sent their completed *Love Bank Inventories* to me every three months. Their scores ranged between 2.4 and 2.8, indicating that they were in love with each other throughout the year. So when we came together for the final session, I was expecting them to be very happy with their marriage and I was not disappointed.

For this final session, I invited them to come into my office together.

The counseling experience of Amy and Jack was essentially educational. But as with every effective educational program, they had to practice what they learned before it would change their lives.

They had learned a basic model for marriage that encouraged Love Bank deposits and discouraged withdrawals. This simple concept helped them understand the value of meeting each other's important emotional needs, which made the most Love Bank deposits. They could also see why making decisions with each other's feelings and interests in mind would help them both make deposits into each other's Love Bank, instead of into only one of their Love Banks, and would avoid withdrawals altogether. Finally, they could see why mutual respect would not only help resolve their conflicts but also keep Love Bank balances healthy.

During their final session, Amy and Jack took turns bringing me up to date on how the year had gone for them. They had learned to live together as a team, and it was a very romantic team at that.

At first, they had thought that scheduling fifteen hours a week to work on their marriage would not be sustainable. They had planned to do it only while counseling with me to solve their problems with sex. But now they realized that it wasn't as difficult as they thought it would be, even though they both had full-time jobs. They had learned to be more efficient with their time. And they could also see how their love for each other depended on it.

They now had the tools to solve just about any marital problem that they would encounter. They had already tried resolving other conflicts and they did it with great success. The Policy of Joint Agreement had helped motivate them to discuss their conflicts rather than argue about them, because an enthusiastic agreement cannot be reached by arguing.

They also saw the wisdom in sticking with me for about two years. With my looking over their shoulder, they were motivated to practice new behavior long enough for it to become almost effortless for them.

As our session ended, I walked them both to the waiting room, and this time no appointment card was necessary. They were now on their own.

While my program for recovery works when it's followed, Amy and Jack get 95 percent of the credit for their success because they followed the program. I had explained after the first session that I would not counsel them if they didn't follow the assignments, and so they took each assignment very seriously. If they had not done so, I would have been wasting my time and their money.

Your job is to point couples in the right direction and to hold them accountable. The program I've described in this book will take them to a passionate and fulfilling marriage if they're willing to follow that path.

Appendix A

Love Bank Inventory

Copyright © 1989 by Willard F. Harley, Jr.

Instructions: Indicate how much you agree or disagree with each of the following statements by circling the appropriate number. Since all answers will reflect your feelings toward _____, do not write his or her name in each blank.

1. I usually experience a good feeling whenever I think about _____.

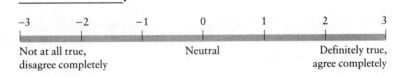

| −3 | −2 | −1 | 0 | 1 | 2 | 3 |

Not at all true, disagree completely   Neutral   Definitely true, agree completely

2. I enjoy being with _____ more than anyone else.

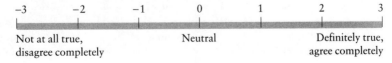

| −3 | −2 | −1 | 0 | 1 | 2 | 3 |

Not at all true, disagree completely   Neutral   Definitely true, agree completely

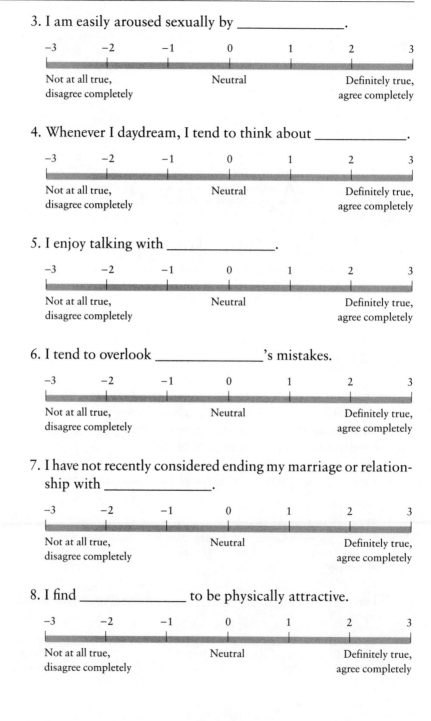

3. I am easily aroused sexually by _____.

| −3 | −2 | −1 | 0 | 1 | 2 | 3 |

Not at all true,   Neutral   Definitely true,
disagree completely   agree completely

4. Whenever I daydream, I tend to think about _____.

| −3 | −2 | −1 | 0 | 1 | 2 | 3 |

Not at all true,   Neutral   Definitely true,
disagree completely   agree completely

5. I enjoy talking with _____.

| −3 | −2 | −1 | 0 | 1 | 2 | 3 |

Not at all true,   Neutral   Definitely true,
disagree completely   agree completely

6. I tend to overlook _____'s mistakes.

| −3 | −2 | −1 | 0 | 1 | 2 | 3 |

Not at all true,   Neutral   Definitely true,
disagree completely   agree completely

7. I have not recently considered ending my marriage or relationship with _____.

| −3 | −2 | −1 | 0 | 1 | 2 | 3 |

Not at all true,   Neutral   Definitely true,
disagree completely   agree completely

8. I find _____ to be physically attractive.

| −3 | −2 | −1 | 0 | 1 | 2 | 3 |

Not at all true,   Neutral   Definitely true,
disagree completely   agree completely

9. I enjoy _____'s sense of humor.

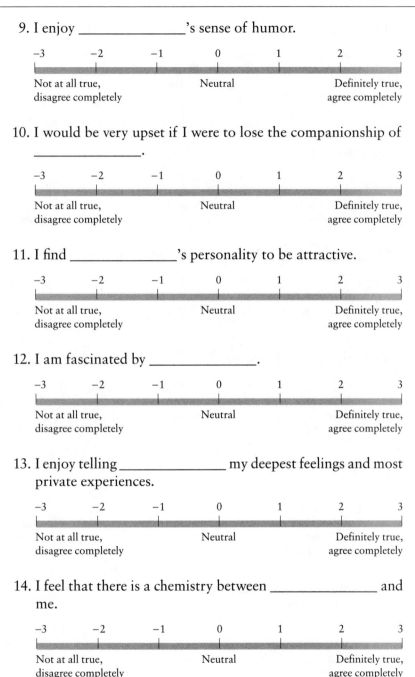

```
-3          -2          -1          0          1          2          3
Not at all true,                 Neutral              Definitely true,
disagree completely                                   agree completely
```

10. I would be very upset if I were to lose the companionship of

_____.

```
-3          -2          -1          0          1          2          3
Not at all true,                 Neutral              Definitely true,
disagree completely                                   agree completely
```

11. I find _____'s personality to be attractive.

```
-3          -2          -1          0          1          2          3
Not at all true,                 Neutral              Definitely true,
disagree completely                                   agree completely
```

12. I am fascinated by _____.

```
-3          -2          -1          0          1          2          3
Not at all true,                 Neutral              Definitely true,
disagree completely                                   agree completely
```

13. I enjoy telling _____ my deepest feelings and most private experiences.

```
-3          -2          -1          0          1          2          3
Not at all true,                 Neutral              Definitely true,
disagree completely                                   agree completely
```

14. I feel that there is a chemistry between _____ and me.

```
-3          -2          -1          0          1          2          3
Not at all true,                 Neutral              Definitely true,
disagree completely                                   agree completely
```

15. _____ brings out the best in me.

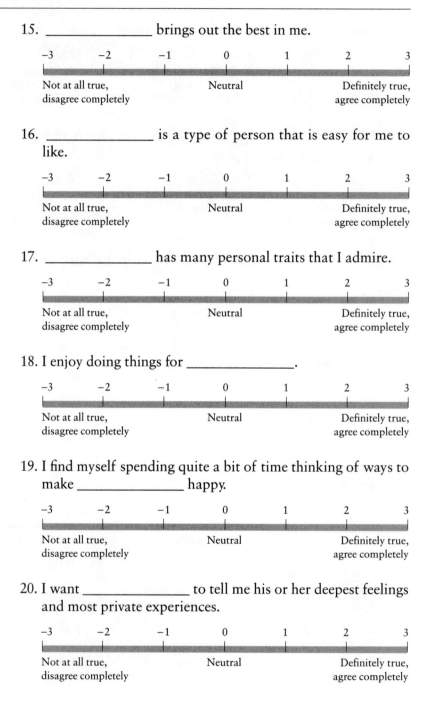

−3   −2   −1   0   1   2   3

Not at all true,   Neutral   Definitely true,
disagree completely   agree completely

16. _____ is a type of person that is easy for me to like.

−3   −2   −1   0   1   2   3

Not at all true,   Neutral   Definitely true,
disagree completely   agree completely

17. _____ has many personal traits that I admire.

−3   −2   −1   0   1   2   3

Not at all true,   Neutral   Definitely true,
disagree completely   agree completely

18. I enjoy doing things for _____.

−3   −2   −1   0   1   2   3

Not at all true,   Neutral   Definitely true,
disagree completely   agree completely

19. I find myself spending quite a bit of time thinking of ways to make _____ happy.

−3   −2   −1   0   1   2   3

Not at all true,   Neutral   Definitely true,
disagree completely   agree completely

20. I want _____ to tell me his or her deepest feelings and most private experiences.

−3   −2   −1   0   1   2   3

Not at all true,   Neutral   Definitely true,
disagree completely   agree completely

21. I am in love with _____.

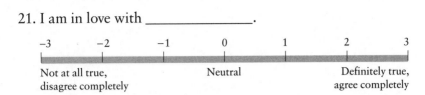

Not at all true,   Neutral   Definitely true,
disagree completely   agree completely

Finding the Love Bank Quotient

First, add the scores for items 1 through 20 (do not include item 21). Then divide that score by 20, the number of items, to obtain the Love Bank Quotient. If the items were answered correctly, the Love Bank Quotient will be within one point of the answer to item 21. My experience with this inventory leads me to conclude that a quotient of 1.8 or greater is obtained when a person is "in love."

Total score of items 1–20: _____

Total score divided by 20: _____ (Love Bank Quotient)

Appendix B

Memorandum of Agreement

THIS AGREEMENT is made this _____ day of _____, 20____, between _____, hereinafter called "Husband," and _____, hereinafter called "Wife," whereby it is mutually agreed:

I. The Husband and Wife will avoid being the cause of each other's pain or discomfort by protecting each other from their own thoughtless decisions and Love Busters:

A. To avoid making thoughtless decisions, the Husband and Wife agree to follow the Policy of Joint Agreement: Never do anything without an enthusiastic agreement between you and your spouse. This policy guarantees that one spouse will not gain at the other's expense.

B. To avoid thoughtless behavior, the Husband and Wife agree to protect each other from the following Love Busters:

1. Selfish Demands: Attempts to force the other to do something with implied threat of punishment if he or she refuses.

2. Disrespectful Judgments: Attempts to change the other's attitudes, beliefs, and behavior by trying to force his or

her way of thinking through lectures, ridicule, threats, and other means.

3. Angry Outbursts: Deliberate attempts to hurt the other spouse because of anger, usually in the form of verbal or physical attacks.

4. Dishonesty: Failure to reveal to the other spouse correct information about emotional reactions, personal history, daily activities, and plans for the future.

5. Annoying Habits: Habits that unintentionally cause the other spouse to be unhappy.

6. Independent Behavior: The conduct of one spouse that is conceived and executed as if the other spouse does not exist. It is usually scheduled and requires planning.

C. If Selfish Demands, Disrespectful Judgments, Angry Outbursts, Dishonesty, Annoying Habits, or Independent Behavior occur, the Husband and Wife agree to follow a plan that identifies them, investigates their causes, keeps a record of their occurrences, and eliminates the behavior.

The Husband will make a special effort to overcome the following:

1. _____

2. _____

3. _____

4. _____

5. _____

6. _____

The Wife will make a special effort to overcome the following:

1. _____

2. _____

3. _____

4. _____

5. _____

6. _____

II. The Husband and Wife agree to meet each other's most important emotional needs.
   A. The Husband and Wife will identify their most important
   emotional needs and select five that are most important to
   the Husband and five that are most important to the Wife.
   These needs may include the following:
      1. Affection: A craving for the expression of care in words,
         cards, gifts, hugs and kisses, courtesies, and other sym-
         bols of care.
      2. Sexual Fulfillment: A craving for sexual experiences.
      3. Conversation: A craving to talk with someone about
         events of the day, feelings and reactions, opinions, and
         plans for the future.
      4. Recreational Companionship: A craving for recreational
         activities with a companion.
      5. Honesty and Openness: A craving for truthful expres-
         sion of feelings, events of the past, daily activities, and
         plans for the future.
      6. Physical Attractiveness: A craving for those with an
         attractive appearance.
      7. Financial Support: A craving to be provided with
         housing, food, clothing, and other essential aspects of
         life.
      8. Domestic Support: A craving for help and/or manage-
         ment of household tasks and child care.
      9. Family Commitment: A craving for help with the moral
         and educational development of one's children.
     10. Admiration: A craving to be valued, appreciated, and
         respected.

The Husband will learn to meet the following emotional needs of the Wife:

1. _____

2. _____

3. _____

4. _____

5. _____

The Wife will learn to meet the following emotional needs of the Husband:

1. _____

2. _____

3. _____

4. _____

5. _____

    B. The Husband and Wife agree to create and follow a plan to help form the new habits that will meet their spouse's five emotional needs.

    C. The Husband and Wife will evaluate the success of their plans, create new plans if the first are unsuccessful, and learn to meet new emotional needs if their spouse replaces any of the original five with a new emotional need. They will meet every month, quarter, year (circle one) to review this agreement and change it if needed.

III. The Husband and Wife agree to take time to give their spouse undivided attention. They will do this by:

    A. Insuring privacy, planning time together that does not include children, relatives, or friends to make undivided attention possible.

B. Using the time together to meet the emotional needs of Affection, Sexual Fulfillment, Conversation, and Recreational Companionship.

C. Committing to spend the number of hours together that reflect the quality of the marriage: Fifteen hours each week if the marriage is mutually satisfying and more time if marital dissatisfaction is reported by either spouse.

D. Scheduling time for undivided attention prior to each week and keeping a record of the actual time spent.

IN WITNESS WHEREOF, the parties hereto have signed this agreement on the day and year first above written:

_____   _____

Husband   Wife

Appendix C

Telephone Counseling

I n 1989, when *His Needs, Her Needs* became a bestseller, couples living outside of Minnesota would fly to the Twin Cities to see me for marriage counseling. They would stay for a week of intensive counseling, and then I would follow up with telephone counseling after they returned home.

This arrangement worked very well for those who could afford to make the trip, but it was expensive when you consider the time off from work and the expense for travel, hotel, and meals. Some couples spent more than three thousand dollars for the week they were here, not counting my counseling fee.

In the interest of economy, I began suggesting to couples wanting to travel here for a week of face-to-face counseling that they consider telephone counseling instead. The intake interview and the diagnostic assessment were done by telephone, and questionnaires were delivered by fax. After a few couples tried it, we were all quite surprised to discover that telephone counseling from start to finish worked just as well as face-to-face counseling. Before long, I and many other counselors in my clinic had ever-increasing numbers of clients whom we counseled by telephone. By 1991 most of my counseling was by telephone, and from 1993 on, all of it has been that way.

The advantages of telephone counseling over in-office, face-to-face counseling are startling. The primary advantage is that you can counsel a couple who has no counselors available in their area. Some communities have no trained marriage counselors, and telephone counseling is the only way for them to get help. But even in large metropolitan areas, it is sometimes difficult for couples to find someone trained in a particular method that they trust.

The convenience and privacy of the telephone are also tremendous advantages. Getting to and from a counseling office can sometimes take couples hours, and they never know whom they'll meet in the waiting room. Telephone counseling, on the other hand, does not even require a babysitter. Most of my clients are able to entertain their children with a video while they are talking to me.

The idea that a counselor's physical presence is essential to counseling success is simply not true. In fact I've discovered that I can help people by telephone whom I could never have reached in person. They were either too embarrassed to come to my office or not motivated enough to make the trip. But by telephone they get all the help they need with complete privacy and very little initial effort. And the results are dramatic.

Of course rebuilding a marriage takes effort. There are questionnaires to complete that help couples discover their weaknesses in marriage. And couples must discipline themselves to learn habits that meet each other's emotional needs and overcome habits that hurt each other. Couples have to stick to the program until it's completed. But the counseling itself requires very little effort when done by telephone.

The single most significant drawback to telephone counseling, however, is that few insurance plans pay for it. Unless you see a couple face-to-face, you are unlikely to receive third-party reimbursement. So throughout this book, I've assumed that you counsel face-to-face in an office setting. But if the couples you counsel are not covered by insurance, consider telephone counseling as a very effective alternative to face-to-face counseling.

Notes

1. Ivan P. Pavlov, *Conditioned Reflexes*, trans. G. V. Anrep (London: Oxford University Press, 1927).

2. Willard F. Harley, Jr., *His Needs, Her Needs: Building an Affair-Proof Marriage* (Grand Rapids: Revell, 1986, 2001).

3. Ron R. Lee, "Best Books for a Better Marriage: Reader's Survey," *Marriage Partnership*, spring 1998.

4. Lynn Hanacek Gravel, *Americans and Marriage: National Survey of U.S. Adults* (Barna Research Group, 2001).

5. Julie D. Braswell, "The Impact of Reading a Self-Help Book on the Topic of Gender Differences on One's Perceived Quality of Marriage" (doctoral diss., Azusa Pacific University, 1998).

6. M. E. P. Seligman, "The Effectiveness of Psychotherapy: The Consumer Reports Study," *American Psychologist* 50 (1995): 965–74.

7. Willard F. Harley, Jr., *Five Steps to Romantic Love: A Workbook for Readers of Love Busters and His Needs, Her Needs* (Grand Rapids: Revell, 1993, 2009); Willard F. Harley, Jr., *Love Busters: Protecting Your Marriage from Habits That Destroy Romantic Love* (Grand Rapids: Revell, 1992, 2008).

Index

abuse, 92
  angry outbursts as, 96–98
  disrespect as, 95–96
  overcoming, 98–99
  physical, 38, 103
  selfish demands as, 92–94
accountability
  of marriage coach, 42, 166
  of spouses, 53, 69, 71, 107, 140, 150, 166
  to weight loss coach, 57, 58
activities, recreational, 55–56
admiration, 61–63
Admiration Inventory, 62
Admiration Worksheet, 63
advocate, marriage coach as, 37
affair(s), 80, 94, 102
affection, 66–68, 80
  in case study, 152
Affection Inventory, 67
  in case study, 140, 142
Affection Worksheet, 67
  in case study, 144, 148, 153, 155, 158, 162
affordable budget, 74
anger management, 38
angry outbursts, 96–98
annoying habits, 104–7
Annoying Habits Inventory, 104, 106
Annoying Habits Worksheet, 107
apathetic swamps, 24–25
assessment, 27, 28–30, 50, 72, 90
  forms, 27; *see also* Marriage Builders
    website

in case study, 124–36
  of Amy, 125–28
  of Jack, 129–31
  time required to complete, 124, 135–36
assignments, 30, 42, 124, 133, 166
  in case study, 134–36, 138, 140, 142, 143
assumptions, 10, 12, 111
  basic, for marital satisfaction, 15–16, 44,
    49, 132

behavior, changing, 94, 98, 142, 147, 149
  practicing new, 150–62, 166
  See also habits
being in love, 79
blaming, 97, 122
brain
  neurophysiological differences in, 104–5
  development in children, 161
brainstorming, 115

career choices, 110, 116–17
chemical dependency, 38
children
  discipline of, 110, 116, 141
    in case study, 143, 153–55, 156, 160–62
  teaching and development of, 75, 87, 117,
    118, 162
  and their care, 59, 83
coach, coaching, marriage, 25
  ability to motivate, 25, 86
  dealing with violence in marriage, 97–98
  definition of, 25, 36

importance of, 34–35
postponing sessions, 135
and resistance to motivation, 36–42, 50
setting goals, 131–33
skills of, 37–42, 137
task of, 35–36
by telephone, 121, 179–80
treatment plan (in case study), 133–36
See also therapists
common sense, 10
communication skills, 12
compatibility
effect of annoying habits on, 104–7
effect of dishonesty on, 101–4
effect of independent behavior on, 110
complaints, 105–6, 139, 160
conditioned response, 16
conditioned stimulus, 16
conditioning, 16
confession of mistakes, 71
confidence and marriage coach, 40–41
confidentiality policies, 26, 122
conflict resolution, 12, 70, 91, 111–12, 116–18
in case study, 151–52, 153, 156–68, 160–62,
163
contracts, 26, 122
control, 92
angry outbursts as, 96–98
disrespect as, 95–96
overcoming, 98–99
selfish demands as, 92–94
conversation, 68–70, 80
content of, 68–69
enemies of, 69
etiquette of, 69
creative wilderness, 24
crisis, 24, 31
criticism, 62, 106, 115, 160
culture
changes in, 11, 59
values in, 109

defensiveness, 138, 139
demand
appropriateness of, during spouse's affair, 94
definition of, 93
dictator strategy, 92
discharge, 31–32, 165–66
preparing for, 162–65

dishonesty, 70, 80, 101–4
motives for, 71
Dishonesty Inventory, 71
Dishonesty Worksheet, 71
disrespect, 95, 115
disrespectful judgments, 53, 94–96, 103
treatment for (in case study), 138–40, 145,
150
Disrespectful Judgments Inventory, 96
in case study, 138
Disrespectful Judgments Worksheet, 96
in case study, 141, 144, 148, 150, 151, 153,
154, 158, 162, 163, 165
division of labor, 59, 60
domestic support, 58–61

effectiveness of treatment strategy, 21, 30; *see
also* progress
emotional barriers, creation of, 70
emotional minefields, 23–24
emotional need(s), 21, 37, 165
definition of, 49
identifying, 35
important, 49–51
in case study, 132, 133, 135, 140
for men, 51–63; see also names of needs
for women, 66–76; see also names of
needs
intimate, 80–82, 83, 84–85, 86; *see also
names of needs*
and mutual enjoyment, 74
rationality of, 73
Emotional Needs Questionnaire (ENQ), 27,
50, 58, 80
in case study, 123, 126, 129, 133
encouragement, by therapist, 26–27
enemies of good conversation, 69
ethical issues in training and counseling, 18,
35, 44
excess weight, 57
sensitivity in addressing, 58
exclusivity
recreational, 56
sexual, 53

family commitment, 75–76, 83; *see also* qual-
ity family time
Family Commitment Inventory, 75
Family Commitment Worksheet, 76

feedback form, 37
  questions to include, 38, 39, 40, 41, 42
  what it tells marriage coach, 43
financial planning, 110, 116, 117, 141
  in case study, 143, 145, 148
financial support, 72–75
Financial Support Inventory: Needs and Wants Budget, 73
finding best solution, 115–16. *See also* negotiation; problem solving strategies
Five Steps to Romantic Love (Harley), 92, 164–65
  assignments in (case study), 134, 135, 140, 144
forms
  assessment, 27
  downloadable, 27–28, 55
  intake, 123–24
  review of, 28
  use of (in case study), 138–39, 141–44, 159
friends, 83, 110, 116, 141
Friends and Enemies of Good Conversation Inventory, 68
Friends and Enemies of Good Conversation Worksheet, 69

goals for treatment, 28–29, 93, 131–33
Golden Rule (Luke 6:31), 50

habits
  annoying, 104–7
  developing new, 98, 106–7, 118, 134, 147, 149, 154; *see also* behavior, changing
  thoughtless, 90–91
Her Household Responsibilities, 60
His Household Responsibilities, 60
His Needs, Her Needs (Harley), 16, 18, 19, 28, 134, 164–65
  assignments in (case study), 140, 142, 143–44, 162, 163
honesty
  and marriage coach, 38–39
  and openness in marriage, 70–72
Household Responsibilities Inventory, 59–60
humor, 150–51, 151–52

important emotional needs. *See* emotional need(s), important
income, reasonable, 73

independent behavior, 109–11
insurance, 26, 122, 180
intake, 25–28, 122–23
intimacy, 80
intimate emotional needs. *See* emotional need(s), intimate
irresistible husband, 76–77
irresistible wife, 63–63

Likert scale
  consistency of, 125–26, 129–30
  definition of, 125
love
  being in, 79
  sacrificial, 10, 12
  unconditional, 10, 12, 17
Love Bank, the, 15–16, 132
  balances in, 32, 35, 43, 81, 89, 113
  measurement of, 19–20, 43
  deposits in, 84, 165
    for men, 51–64
    for women, 65–76
  withdrawals from, 88, 89–90, 96, 105, 110, 132, 157
  categories of, 91; see also names of categories
Love Bank Inventory (LBI), 20, 27, 29, 30
  in case study, 124, 133, 165, 166
    Amy, 127–28, 145, 153, 156, 160, 163
    Jack, 131, 147, 152, 156, 164
  copy of, 167–71
  as indicator of therapist's performance, 43
Love Busters, 21, 28, 90–91
  angry outbursts, 96–97
  annoying habits, 104–7
  dishonesty, 70, 101–4
  disrespect, 95
  identifying, 35, 90
  independent behavior, 109
  selfishness, 93–94
Love Busters (Harley), 94, 96, 98, 164–65
  assignments in (case study), 134, 138
Love Busters Questionnaire (LBQ), 27, 90
  in case study, 123, 126, 129–30, 135
love units, 15, 35, 49

Marital Counseling History Questionnaire (MCHQ), 27, 39
  in case study, 124, 127–28

Marital Problems Analysis (MPA), 27
in case study, 124, 127, 130
marital satisfaction, 12, 85, 102
basic assumption for, 15–16, 44, 49
model(s) of, 10, 15, 39
marriage
abusive consequences in, 93
commitment in, 10, 12, 17, 164–65
compatibility
effect of dishonesty on, 101–4
effect of annoying habits on, 104–7
effect of independent behavior on, 110
control in, effect of, 93
dealing with violence in, 97–98, 103
obstacles to good, 23–25
as partnership of equals, 92–93, 111
quality of, 85–86
Marriage Builders website, 27–28, 55
marriage coach. *See* coach, coaching, marriage
Memorandum of Agreement (MOA), 29,
173–77
in case study, 128, 131, 133
men, important emotional needs of, 51–63
money. *See* financial planning
motivation
lack of, 60–61, 86
and resistance to, 36–42, 50
role of, 29, 30, 35

needs budget, 73–74
negative balances in Love Bank, 17, 32,
81–82, 89, 92, 98, 132
negative feedback loop, 17–18, 81
negotiation, 93, 98, 111, 112
in case study, 151
guidelines for, 113–16

objectives, 84–85
observation, 10
oppositional behavior, 161
organization and professionalism of marriage
coach, 41–42, 137

partnership of equals, marriage as, 92–93, 111
Pavlov, Ivan P., 16
Personal History Questionnaire (PHQ), 27, 72
in case study, 124, 127, 131, 133
personal satisfaction, 74
Physical Appearance Inventory, 57

physical attractiveness, 56–58
Policy of Joint Agreement, 111–12, 116, 153,
157, 161, 163, 164, 166
Policy of Radical Honesty, 70–71, 101–2, 114
Policy of Undivided Attention, 82–86, 164
positive balances in Love Bank, 17, 32, 91, 132
practicing new behaviors (in case study),
150–62
respectful persuasion, 154–55
resolving conflict, 151–52, 160–62
showing affection, 152
precounseling inquiry, 26
predictability of scientific model, 9
presenting complaint or problem, 127, 131
privacy, 83–84
problem solving strategies, 114, 157
effective, 94, 111
thoughtless, 91–98
progress
documentation or measurement of, 20–21,
31, 42, 49, 67, 69
use of forms to document (in case study),
138–39, 141–42, 145, 159
punctuality, 27, 42

quality family time, 75, 117, 162, 163; *see also*
family commitment
Quality Family Time Graph, 76, 87

ranking of emotional needs, 50, 125
rationalization, 95
recreational companionship, 54–56, 80
Recreational Companionship Worksheet, 56
Recreational Enjoyment Inventory, 55
referrals, 41, 122
registration forms, 26, 122
relatives, 83, 110, 116, 141
in case study, 143, 148, 151–53, 157, 162
resentment, 84, 112–13, 157–58
respect, 94, 166
Respectful Judgments Inventory, 135
respectful persuasion, 96, 143
in case study, 145, 154–55
Respectful Persuasion Worksheet, 96
in case study, 141, 144, 148, 151, 153, 158,
160, 162, 163, 165
responsibility, acknowledging personal, 97
restraining order, 97
romantic love, 13–14

romantic love threshold, 16, 17, 32, 49, 62, 65, 132
romantic relationship, definition of, 79

sacrificial love, 10
scientific evidence for effectiveness of method, 18–19
scientific model, 9
selfish demands, 92–94
Selfish Demands Inventory, 93–94
Selfish Demands Worksheet, 94
selfishness, 11, 93–94
selflessness, 11
separation, 97
sequence of therapy, 25–32
sessions
  length of, 26–27, 137
  postponing, 135
  scheduling, 124
setting goals, 131–33
setting ground rules, 114
sex, 110, 117
sexual availability and responsiveness, mutual, 53–54
sexual exclusivity, 53–54
Sexual Experience Inventory, 52
  in case study, 144, 146
Sexual Experience Worksheet, 52
  in case study, 144
sexual fulfillment, 51–54, 80, 143
Sexual Fulfillment Inventory, 52
Sexual Fulfillment Worksheet, 52
sexual incompatibility, 53
sexual response, stages of, 52
simplicity of scientific model, 9
spontaneous recovery, 154–55
strategies of marriage coaching, 24
Strategy to Discover the Five Stages of Sexual Experience, 52
  in case study, 144
Strategy to Meet the Need of Admiration, 62
Strategy to Meet the Need of Affection, 67
  in case study, 140
Strategy to Meet the Need of Conversation, 69
Strategy to Meet the Need of Family Commitment, 76
Strategy to Meet the Need of Physical Attractiveness, 57

Strategy to Meet the Need of Recreational Companionship, 56
Strategy to Meet the Need of Sexual Fulfillment, 52
Strategy to Overcome Annoying Habits, 106
Strategy to Overcome Dishonesty, 71
Strategy to Replace Disrespectful Judgments with Respectful Persuasion, 96
  in case study, 135, 138
Strategy to Replace Selfish Demands with Thoughtful Requests, 94
subject knowledge and marriage coach, 39–40

telephone counseling, 121, 179–80
therapeutic control, 43–44
therapists
  dealing with violence in marriage, 97–98
  ethical issues in training, 18, 35, 44
  mediation by, 31
  skills of, 24–25
  training of, 18, 72
  See also coach, coaching, marriage
therapy, sequence of, 25–32
thoughtful request, 93
Thoughtful Requests Worksheet, 94
time
  management, 110, 116–17, 141, 166
  scheduling, 87–88
  weekly commitment, for couples, 28, 29, 82, 85–86, 124, 133–34
Time for Undivided Attention Graph, 87
Time for Undivided Attention Worksheet, 29, 87
  in case study, 134, 138, 139, 141, 144, 148, 150, 153, 158, 162, 165
treatment
  and practice, 30–31
  strategy, effectiveness of, 21, 30
    for affection, 141–44
    in case study, 133–36
    for disrespectful judgments, 138–40
    for sexual fulfillment, 144–48
trust
  importance of, in marriage, 70, 102
  and marriage coach, 37–38

unconditional love, 10, 17
unconditioned response, 16
unconditioned stimulus, 16

understanding another's perspective, 114–15
undivided attention, 29, 69, 117, 133–34, 138
   in case study, 139, 141, 144, 145, 158
Undivided Attention Worksheet, 29

violence
   and discipline of children, 155
   in marriage, 97–98, 103
vocational counseling and training, 73

wants budget, 74
weight, excess, 57
   sensitivity in addressing, 58
weight loss plan, 57
women, important emotional needs of, 66–76

Dr. Willard F. Harley, Jr., is a nationally acclaimed clinical psychologist, marriage counselor, and bestselling author. His popular website, www.marriagebuilders.com, offers practical solutions to almost any marital problem. Dr. Harley and his wife, Joyce, host a three-hour radio call-in show called *Marriage Builders Radio*, as well as Marriage Builders Weekend conferences. They live in White Bear Lake, Minnesota.

THE RESOURCE EVERY COUPLE NEEDS

In this classic book, Dr. Willard F. Harley, Jr. identifies the ten most vital needs of women and men and shows husbands and wives how to satisfy those needs in their spouses.

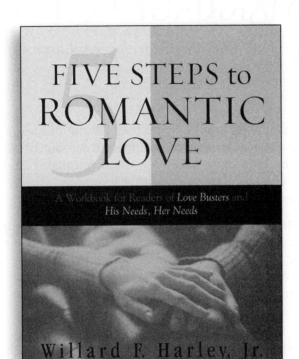

MARRIAGE BUILDERS ®
Building Marriages to Last a Lifetime

Why do people fall in love? Why do they fall out of love? What do they want most in marriage? What drives them out of marriage? How can a bad marriage become a great marriage? Dr. Harley's basic concepts address these and other important aspects of marriage building.

At www.marriagebuilders.com, Dr. Harley introduces visitors to some of the best ways to overcome marital conflicts and some of the quickest ways to restore love. From the pages of "Basic Concepts" and articles by Dr. Harley to the archives for his weekly Q&A columns and information about upcoming seminars, this site is packed with useful material.

Let Marriage Builders™ help you build a marriage to last a lifetime!
www.marriagebuilders.com